*F*lying *C*olours 3

Workbook

Judy Garton-Sprenger   **Simon Greenall**

Heinemann English Language Teaching
A division of Heinemann Publishers (Oxford) Ltd
Halley Court, Jordan Hill,
Oxford OX2 8EJ

OXFORD   MADRID   ATHENS
PARIS   FLORENCE   PRAGUE
SÃO PAULO   CHICAGO   MELBOURNE
AUCKLAND   SINGAPORE   TOKYO
GABORONE   JOHANNESBURG
PORTSMOUTH (NH)   IBADAN

ISBN 435 28321 9

© Judy Garton-Sprenger and Simon Greenall 1992
First published 1992

Designed by Susan Clarke
Cover illustration by Lo Cole
Illustrations by David Cuzik, Ian Dicks, Hardlines,
Michael Salter

While every effort has been made to trace the owners
of copyright material in this book, there have been
some cases where the publishers have been unable to
contact the owners. We should be grateful to hear
from anyone who recognises their copyright material
and who is unacknowledged. We shall be pleased to
make the necessary amendments in future editions of
the book.

Typeset in 11/13 Garamond Original Roman by
Colset Ltd, Singapore
Printed and bound in Great Britain by
Thomson Litho Ltd,
East Kilbride, Scotland

94 95 96 10 9 8 7 6 5 4 3

While every effort has been made to trace the owners of copyright material in
this book, there have been some cases where the publishers have been unable
to contact the owners. We should be grateful to hear from anyone who
recognises their copyright material and who is unacknowledged. We shall be
pleased to make the necessary amendments in future editions of the book.

The authors and publishers are grateful to the following for their permission to
use copyright material in this book.

p5 The Observer (extract slightly adapted from original by Daphne Glazer
[6.1.91]); p10 Cosmopolitan, UK edition (extract taken from 'It's Review Time'
[November 1988]); p11 The Spectator (cartoon [16.12.89]); p15 Penguin Books
Ltd (quotations 1–5 taken from *The Penguin Dictionary of Modern Humorous
Quotations* [1986]); p15 Longman (quotations 6–12 taken from *Contradictory
Quotations, Longman Pocket Companion Series* [1983]); p15 The Spectator
(cartoon [16.12.89]); p19 Punch (cartoon [25.3.88]); p21 The Independent
(extract adapted from original by Tim Jackson [3.11.90]); p23 The Observer
(extract adapted from advertising copy for the British Airports Authority by
Desmond Morris [4.12.88]); p27 Ringpress Books Ltd (extract from *All Our
Children* by Judith and Martin Woodhead); p29 © Peter Mayle 1989 (extract
from *A Year in Provence* by Peter Mayle [Hamish Hamilton 1989, Pan 1990]);
p31 The Independent (extract adapted from 'An On-Call Marsupial' by Rebecca
Hodson [1991]); p33 The Guardian (extract adapted from original first published
in EG Supplement [6.11.90]); p35 The Independent (extracts taken from original
by Frank Barrett [7.9.91]); p39 © Simon Callow 1984 (extract adapted from
Being an Actor by Simon Callow [Methuen 1984, Penguin 1985] reprinted by
permission of Methuen, London); p41 © Malcolm Bradbury 1975 (extracts from
The History Man by Malcolm Bradbury [Secker & Warburg 1975] reprinted by
permission of Martin Secker & Warburg Ltd); p43 The Guardian (extract
adapted from original by Wendy Berliner [2.7.91]); p45 The Observer (extracts
adapted from original by Peter Corrigan [6.1.91]); p53 Usborne Publishing Ltd,
London (extract from *Usborne Introduction to Politics and Government* by Janet
Cook and Stephen Kirby [1986]); p55 Lena Pallin/Adam Bromberg ('A New Life'
by Slawomir Mrozek published in *The European* [18–20 January 1991]); p59
Wayland (Publishers) Ltd (extracts taken from *Transport: Looking Back Series* by
Nigel Flynn); p67 © Mica Management Resources Inc 1990 (extracts from
'Sequence Patterns' in *I am right – You are wrong* by Edward de Bono [Viking
1990, Penguin 1991]); p69 © YOU magazine/Solo (extract from original YOU
magazine feature [4.10.87]); pp71, 77 John May, Greenpeace Books (story
adapted from original in Curious Facts Magazine no 3).

CONTENTS

① Complete the passage with verbs from the list below. Use the present perfect or past simple tense.

be   become   bring   change   come   enjoy
expect   finish   keep   make   pay   play   see
star   take over   win

007 Licensed to Kill

James Bond first **1** .... to the cinema screen in *Dr No* in 1962, and he **2** .... excitement and adventure to audiences round the world ever since. Over 1.75 billion people **3** .... to see 007 at the cinema, and more than half the population of the world **4** .... a Bond movie at one time or another.

So far, there **5** .... four different James Bonds. No one **6** .... *Dr No* to be so successful, but Sean Connery soon **7** .... world famous as the first 007. He **8** .... in six Bond films before Roger Moore **9** .... the role in 1973 with *Live and Let Die*. George Lazenby also **10** .... Bond in 1969 in the not-so-successful *On Her Majesty's Secret Service*. And in 1987, Timothy Dalton **11** .... his first appearance as 007 in *The Living Daylights*, the sixteenth Bond film.

Since 1962, the Bond films **12** .... with the times, and 007 **13** .... up-to-date with politics, space technology – and beautiful women. He **14** .... hearts both on screen and off, and people of all ages **15** .... his adventures. And he **16** .... n't .... yet!

② Put these words in order. Add capital letters and punctuation, and make sentences.

1 to ever concerts do jazz go you

....

2 month we about the a go cinema to once

....

3 wears ever clothes he smart hardly

....

4 nights do do on usually what Saturday you

....

5 never my jeans parents worn have

....

6 English often have you how lessons do

....

③ Write sentences saying what you:

sometimes wear at weekends

....

....

usually have for breakfast

....

....

often do in the evenings

....

....

hardly ever eat

....

....

do every morning

....

....

never wear in the summer

....

....

occasionally read

....

....

do once a year

....

....

4 Read the passage, and then write sentences about things that Ruth used to do.

Five years ago, Ruth lived in a flat in London. She taught physics at a secondary school, and she always cycled to work because she didn't have a car. In the evenings, she usually played squash with friends or watched TV, and on Saturday nights she went out with her boyfriend, Jack.

Now Ruth and Jack are married with two children, and they live in a house in the country. Ruth teaches physics at a technical college and she cycles to work in summer, but in winter she drives. In the evenings, she plays with the children and watches TV, and on Saturday nights she goes out with Jack.

She used to live in a flat in London.

....

....

....

....

....

Now write sentences about four things that Ruth still does.

....

....

....

....

5 Add as many adjectives as you can to this word map.

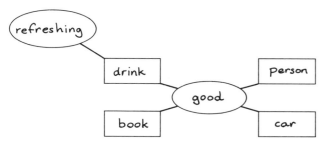

Now make a similar word map with *bad* at the centre.

6 Read the passage below and choose the best title.

a DEAN FOR SALE
b LIVE FAST, DIE YOUNG
c DEATH OF A STAR, BIRTH OF A LEGEND
d TEENAGE TRAGEDY

7 Decide where these phrases can go in the passage.

a as a wild adolescent in *East of Eden*
b to encourage teenagers to save money
c to drink what was to be his last bottle of Coke

James Dean was only 24 when he was killed in a car accident on 30 September 1955. He was driving his new silver-painted Porsche on Highway 46 in California. He had stopped at a truckstop, and minutes later he crashed into a Ford driven by a 23-year-old student called Donald Turnupseed. 'Live fast, die young . . .' was Dean's motto, and it is also a fitting epitaph for his brief life.

He had shot to fame in 1955 when he first appeared on screen; his other two films, *Rebel Without a Cause* and *Giant*, were not released until after his death. But if James Dean was a star in life, in death he became an immortal hero. The young man who was known as 'the first teenager' is still the ultimate symbol of teenage rebellion, even though many young people today have never seen his films.

He is also the centre of an industry worth over $100 million a year and his image has travelled worldwide. You can drink out of a James Dean coffee mug in Sweden, smoke a James Dean pipe in Japan, and choose food from a James Dean menu in Mexico. He appears on towels, T-shirts, tracksuits, sunglasses, cologne bottles, and greetings cards all over the world. And in Britain, the National Westminster Bank even uses his image in advertisements!

1 Complete the sentences saying what you usually do.

1 After writing a letter, ...

....

2 Before going to bed, ...

....

3 After having dinner, ...

....

4 Before going out of the house, ...

....

5 After getting up, ...

....

6 Before taking an exam, ...

....

2 Rewrite each sentence using *before/after* + *-ing*.

1 John Logie Baird went to school in Glasgow and then he worked as a salesman.

After *going to school in Glasgow, John Logie Baird worked as a salesman.*

2 He heard about Marconi's experiments with radio waves and then he tried to transmit a moving picture.

After ....

....

....

3 He experimented for many years and then he invented the television.

Before ....

....

4 He invited some scientists to his workshop and then he demonstrated his invention.

Before ....

....

5 He made the first TV transmission in 1925, and he immediately became famous.

After ....

....

3 Rewrite the sentences in exercise 3 using *after* + past perfect.

1 *After John Logie Baird had been*

....

....

....

2 ....

....

....

3 ....

....

4 ....

....

5 ....

....

❹ **Read the passage opposite. You can look up the underlined words.**

Now find:

1 three different ways of saying *television*

....

2 two adjectives meaning *very unkind*

....

3 an adjective meaning *very bossy*

....

4 a noun meaning *bad dreams*

....

5 a phrase meaning *I do not need*

....

❺ **Write down three reasons why people think the writer should have a TV.**

....

....

....

Write down two reasons why she does not want a TV.

....

....

❻ **Write a title for the passage.**

....

❼ **Think about TV programmes in your country and write down two examples of each category.**

documentaries

....

soap operas

....

game shows

....

news programmes

....

comedy programmes

....

chat shows

....

'How on earth can you survive?' my students say, on discovering my lack of a television set. 'Whatever do you *do* in the evenings?' 'Aren't you bored?'

Friends and acquaintances look serious. 'There are some very good nature programmes . . . it's very educational . . . you're missing a lot,' they say.

From time to time, an official letter arrives demanding the details of my TV set. Two heavy men in suits ring the doorbell and ask me if I possess a television.

I am used to all this and have dismissed it in the past with a show of jocularity, or simply a smile. Recently, however, the pressure to <u>conform</u> has increased.

Three months ago, my husband had an accident and has become temporarily housebound. No sooner had this happened than a renewed <u>onslaught</u> started. 'Oh, you need a telly, he'd feel much better, poor man.'

Two weeks ago a telly arrived and squatted, not plugged in, on our front-room floor for several days. It had been sent by a friend, who didn't feel the need to consult me first.

The telly was returned. Now <u>sniping</u> has given way to full-scale war. How can I be so heartless as to refuse to have a telly? My refusal has even secured us several dinner invitations just to soften me up and make me see that I am in error.

It is thought that I am a domineering harpie of a wife and I am also being cruel to our 10-year-old son by my refusal.

So, what is my defence? We live in a house which has only one sitting-room. Were a TV to be installed, it would mean that it would dominate the entire household. The sound would be all-pervasive.

I am a novelist who also has a full-time job. Far from having a room of my own, I have to fit my writing in odd corners. I mostly write in our bedroom, directly above the front room. There are no extra rooms where one might escape the sound.

I need to write. I feel almost embarrassed to tell people this because they seem so dismissive of it. For me, writing is akin to breathing. I also need to read and to prepare material for my <u>workshops</u>.

What has amazed me is that my decision not to have a TV set is presented as a moral issue, not simply a matter of taste.

'You are <u>depriving</u> your son,' I am <u>told</u>. Depriving him of what? Of a habit of passivity and a constant need to be entertained? Of nightmares because of the violence he has seen on the box?

That I can do without – along with the television set.

1 Write sentences saying whether you can or can't do the following things in your country.

smoke on buses

....

go to school/work in jeans

....

drive in town without wearing a seatbelt

....

ride a bicycle on a motorway

....

get married when you are sixteen

....

2 Complete the sentences with future simple clauses.

1 If you go to bed late, *you'll feel tired* .... *tomorrow.*

2 If you turn on the light, ...

....

3 If you follow the map, ...

....

4 If you break the window, ...

....

5 If you take an umbrella, ...

....

3 Rewrite your sentences in exercise 2.

1 *Go to bed late and you'll feel tired* *tomorrow.*

2 ....

....

3 ....

....

4 ....

....

5 ....

....

4 Match the two halves of these slogans.

1 To make your hair softer, . . .
2 To brighten up your home, . . .
3 To stay ahead in business, . . .
4 To lose weight fast, . . .
5 To travel in style, . . .
6 To end a perfect meal, . . .

a . . . work with Quasar computers.
b . . . serve Cafetine coffee.
c . . . paint the walls with Coverall.
d . . . fly Trans Sky Airlines..
e . . . use Elegance shampoo.
f . . . take Shape-up slimming pills.

1	
2	
3	
4	
5	
6	

5 Rewrite the slogans in exercise 4 using *by* + *-ing.*

1 *Make your hair softer by using* *Elegance shampoo.*

2 ....

....

3 ....

....

4 ....

....

5 ....

....

6 ....

....

6 Write the dialogue in reported speech.

JILL What's the matter?
ROB   The TV isn't working and I want to watch the news.
JILL Can I have a look at it?
ROB   You see, the picture's OK but the sound has gone.
JILL Perhaps there's a transmission fault.
ROB   No, the same thing happened last night.
JILL How long have you had the TV?
ROB   I only bought it last month.
JILL Well, if I were you, I'd take it back to the shop and ask them to repair it.
ROB   I'll take it in on my way to work tomorrow.

7 Read these advertisements and notices. They all contain mistakes. Can you correct them?

1 Wanted – man to take care of cow that does not smoke or drink.

Advert in South Carolina paper

2 Woman wants cleaning three days a week.

Advert in *The Guardian*

3 Don't Kill Your Wife With Work *Let Electricity Do It*

Poster in London

4 We do not tear your clothes with machinery We do it carefully by hand

Sign in laundry window

5 *WANTED – Sports leather coat for lady in perfect condition.*

Advert in *Nippon Times*

6 WANTED, new pair of football boots, for a good young Fox-terrier dog.

Advert in *Our Dogs*

7 *HEADACHES? Let us examine your eyes and help you in removing them.*

Notice in optician's window

8 Lady desires post; domesticated, fond of cooking children.

Advert in weekly paper

9 Wanted, maid for mousework, four in family

Advert in Toronto paper

10 For sale – Baker's business, good trade, large oven, present owner been in it for seventeen years.

Advert in Kent paper

11 ! GREAT SHOE OFFER ! Every pain guaranteed

Advert in provincial paper

Jill asked ....

Rob said ....

....

Jill asked ....

....

Rob explained ....

....

Jill wondered ....

....

Rob told ....

....

Jill asked ....

....

Rob replied ....

....

Jill suggested ....

....

....

Rob said ....

....

Now try to identify and correct the mistakes. Use this list to help you.

a incorrect punctuation
b misprints / spelling mistakes
c words or phrases in the wrong order
d pronouns that refer back to the wrong thing
e missing words

1 Rewrite these sentences in the passive. Use *by* + agent only if necessary.

1 People buy over 20 million newspapers in Britain each day.

....

....

2 Newsagents sell the *Evening Standard* in London.

....

....

3 Over a million people read *The Independent*.

....

....

4 News agencies supply many news items.

....

....

5 Foreign correspondents send in stories from abroad.

....

....

6 The editorial staff select and process the stories.

....

....

7 They now print many newspapers in colour.

....

....

8 The paperboy delivers our newspaper in the morning.

....

....

2 Complete the passage with the past simple active or passive form of the verbs in brackets.

One of the first newspapers **1** (produce) .... by Julius Caesar. When he **2** (become) .... Consul in 60 BC, he **3** (start) .... the *Acta Diurna*, a daily bulletin of government announcements which **4** (put up) .... in the Forum in Rome. But real newspapers only **5** (appear) .... in the eighteenth century. The first regular newspaper **6** (begin) .... publication in Augsburg, Germany, in 1690, and the first daily newspaper, the *Daily Courant*, **7** (publish) .... in London in 1702. But many people **8** (can) .... not read, and as recently as two hundred years ago, most of the news **9** (carry) .... by word of mouth. People **10** (rely) .... on town criers who **11** (pay) .... to shout information as they **12** (walk) .... through the streets.

3 Read these definitions and complete them.

1 The .... of a newspaper or magazine is the number of copies that are sold each time it is produced.

2 A .... newspaper is a paper which is published every day except Sunday.

3 A newspaper .... is someone who is in charge of a newspaper.

4 A financial .... is someone who writes news stories about business and economics.

5 A book .... is an article which describes a new book and gives an opinion of it.

6 A .... is an electronic machine that can quickly make calculations, and store and rearrange information.

❹ **Write definitions of the following people and things.**

1 A journalist ....

   ....

2 The readership of a newspaper ....

   ....

3 A national newspaper ....

   ....

4 A sports correspondent ....

   ....

5 A typewriter ....

   ....

   ....

6 A film review ....

   ....

7 A photographer ....

   ....

❺ **Can you identify the newspaper extracts? Match them with the words below.**

	horoscope
	weather forecast
	book review
	TV guide
	advertisement
	recipe
	crossword puzzle
	sports report
	financial report

❻ **The passive is often used in news reports. Read some news reports in English newspapers, and underline the passive constructions. Think about the context in which they are used.**

1

ACROSS

4   She's from a strange land (6)

7   Chariots sent around for the beans (8)

8   Domestic vessel for drink and dope? (6)

DOWN

1   Has figures out in deep space (5)

2   Is its handle of brushwood? (5)

3   The book of Cats? (4)

---

2 **United feels the pressure**

UNITED Newspapers, owners of the Daily Express and Yorkshire Post, reported a 31% fall in profits to £38.6 million in the six months to end-June.

Turnover was down by a less severe 3% at £411.2 million. The interim dividend is held at 7.5p and the shares rose 11p to 395p.

---

3 AS THOUGH it were a biography, this novel contains the author's thanks to a host of people, ranging from father Kingsley to stepfather-in-law Xan Fielding, from Simon Wiesenthal to Tom Maschler, from Saul Bellow to Clive James. But sadly, this abundance of assistance has not produced the result for which the author must have hoped. Time's Arrow is not a first-rate novel, although it is certainly a fascinating and exhilarating shot at one.

---

4 **South-east tonight:** Showers will die away with skies becoming clearer, so there may be patchy mist and fog by morning. It will be quite a chilly night, **Low:** 8C (46F).

Tomorrow: The mist and fog will clear quickly and it will be a bright day with quite a lot of sunshine, although it will turn more cloudy in the evening. **High:** 17C (63F).

Information supplied by the Met Office

---

5 **SALES ASSISTANT** required for Busy City Stationers. Experience in Stationery & selling preferable. Smart appearance. ALSO

PART-TIME CASHIER required Hours 11.00 - 3.00 Monday to Friday Call Bill Bishop on 071 626 4644

---

6 Heat the oven to 190C/375F/Gas Mark 5. Brush an oven dish with a little of the remaining oil.

Mix the rosemary, garlic, breadcrumbs, salt and plenty of pepper. Coat the fish with the mixture, pressing the crumbs onto the fish with your hands. Wrap a slice of prosciutto around each one and lay in the prepared dish. Dribble over the remaining oil and bake for 15–20 minutes, basting the fish once or twice. Serve from the dish, handing round lemon wedges.

---

7 On Saturday they are at home to League leaders Manchester United. They then face Hajduk Split in the European Cup Winners' Cup first round, second leg, Everton in the League, and Swansea in the return leg of the Rumbelows Cup.

They went into last night's game at Swansea without England captain Gary Lineker and the defeat, to a goal by Jimmy Gilligan two minutes from time, emphasised that without Lineker's lethal touch in the penalty area, Tottenham struggle to score.

8

BBC 1	
6.30	Breakfast News
9.05	Kilroy
9.50	Hot Chefs
10.00	News; Regional News; Weather
10.05	Playdays
10.25	Pingu
10.35	No Kidding With Mike Smith
11.00	News; Regional News; Weather

---

9 **LEO** July 24 to Aug 23

YOU have far more drive than the average human being. As a result you have to work a lot harder because you stand to lose a lot more. You are ambitious and go-getting today but remember to put some time aside for having fun!

❶ Read this article from *Cosmopolitan* magazine, and think about important areas of your life – including learning English! Note down at least one answer to each question.

IT'S REVIEW TIME

Now's the time to evaluate your progress, achievements and disappointments and then set new goals. The easiest and most illuminating way to do this is to write each of the following questions on a separate piece of paper and then note down everything that you think of on each page. Start with your career, and then go on to other important areas of your life – partners, friends, family, social life and hobbies for instance. These are the key questions:

1 What am I doing now that I still want to do in the future?
2 What am I doing now that I don't want to do any more?
3 What am I *not* doing now that I would like to do?
4 What have I done in the past that I know I *never* want to do again?
5 What *should* I be doing that I really want to do?
6 What should I be doing that I *don't* want to do?

Read your notes and highlight your aims. Look for any patterns and decide what you are going to do and by when. Next year's review will be much more positive!

❷ Write sentences based on your answers in exercise 1. Use:
I'm (not) going to . . .
I'm never going to . . . again.
I've decided (not) to . . .
I will/won't . . .

....
....
....
....
....
....
....
....
....
....
....
....

❸ Complete the sentences with a suitable infinitive or *-ing* construction.

1 The nurse was so tired that she couldn't help ....
2 I can't afford .... in expensive restaurants.
3 You really should try .... your bills on time.
4 I really enjoy .... when I'm on holiday.
5 If you want .... , you shouldn't eat between meals.
6 You're not supposed .... in the library.
7 Would you mind .... for a few minutes?
8 When I've finished .... , I'm going to bed.

❹ Write answers using *-ing* constructions and the following phrases:

forget their lines   look after their children
win elections   see the sights   design buildings
be alone in the dark

1 What are architects good at?

....
....

2 What are politicians keen on?

....
....

3 What do actors worry about?

....
....

4 What are children often afraid of?

....
....

5 What are tourists interested in?

....
....

6 What are parents responsible for?

....
....

❺ Complete these sentences with *-ing* constructions.

I'm good at ....

....

I'm proud of ....

....

I'm not keen on ....

....

I'm afraid of ....

....

I'm sorry about ....

....

I'm addicted to ....

....

I'm not interested in ....

....

❻ Complete these conditional sentences with the correct form of the verbs in brackets.

1 If I .... prime minister,
I .... more money on education.
(be, spend)
2 I .... you a lift to the airport if you
.... (give, like)
3 I haven't got her address. If I .... it,
I .... you. (know, tell)
4 Please hurry up! If we ....
late, we .... the beginning of the play.
(be, miss)
5 See you when I get back. And I .... if
I .... time. (write, have)
6 I'm glad I live in a city. If I .... live
in the country, I .... of boredom.
(have to, die)

❼ Complete the sentences with compounds formed with *over* + the words below.

work   eat   sleep   load
priced   weight   cooked   crowded

1 If I don't set my alarm clock,
I'll ....
2 The car is too expensive –
it's ....
3 The village is .... because
of the tourists.
4 If you .... the boat, it'll
sink.
5 I don't like .... vegetables.
6 He needs to take a holiday – he's exhausted
through ....
7 I'm on a diet and I mustn't
....
8 She's not .... – she's very
slim.

*'Miss Nathan, find out what a lifestyle is and then get
me one.'*

❶ Decide which lesson of Unit 1 in the Students'
Book the following words come from.

cartoon complain documentary editor fan
headline lifestyle make-up overwork
performer perfume persuade phobia publish
refreshing rehearsal right-wing satisfaction
slogan subtitled

1 Household names
2 Television talk
3 Campaign
4 Britain in View: The press
5 I'm not going to give up . . .

❷ Complete the sentences with the words in bold.

fun, funny
1 I think Woody Allen is extremely ....
2 Did you have .... at the party?

channels, programmes
3 Britain has two state-owned TV .... : BBC1 and BBC2.
4 BBC2 usually offers more serious ....

advertisement, sign
5 Didn't you see the .... ? It says 'Keep out'.
6 I found my flat through an .... in the local paper.

choose, decide
7 I can't .... whether it's going to rain or not.
8 Will you help me .... a present for my father?

check, control
9 You should .... your written work before handing it in.
10 Some parents find it difficult to .... their children.

❸ Write these words in the correct column, and underline the letters which match the sounds.

afford article audience comic company control country course department drama encourage
gossip laughter local money opera performer programme quality social staff suppose
thoughtful watch worry

/ɑː/	/ʌ/	/ɒ/	/ɔː/	/əʊ/

4 Match the words with the stress patterns.

battery casual delicious distribute episode
financial powerful refreshing rehearsal
reporter subtitled talented

● ● ●   ● ● ●

....

....

....

....

....

....

5 Check how much English you know. Answer yes
(✓), not sure (?) or no (X).

Can you . . .?

remember five adverbs and phrases of
  frequency
use *not any more* and *still*
use infinitive constructions
use gerund constructions after prepositions
  and verbs
use the first conditional
use the second conditional
use the present and past simple passive
use defining relative clauses

Do you know how to . . .?

talk about present opinions, attitudes and
  habits
talk about past opinions, attitudes and
  habits
talk about past experience
describe a sequence of routine actions in
  the present
describe a sequence of actions in the past
express permission and prohibition
report what was said
describe a process
talk about future plans and intentions

Do you know when to use . . .?

the present perfect and the past simple
the past perfect and the past simple
the first and second conditional
active and passive constructions

If you answered *no* to any questions, look at the
STRUCTURES TO LEARN in Lessons 1–5 of your
Students' Book. Write sentences using the
structures.

....

....

....

....

If you answered *not sure* to any questions, write
sentences using the structures.

....

....

....

....

6 Now look at the **STRUCTURES TO LEARN** in
Lessons 1–5 of your Students' Book and check.

Write a few sentences about:

• household names in your country
• television in your country
• your opinion of advertising
• the press in your country
• your future plans and intentions

....

....

....

....

....

....

....

....

....

....

....

....

....

1 Complete the charts.

Present perfect continuous tense

Affirmative

Full form	Short form
I/you/we/they .... been working	I've/you've/we've/ they've .... working
he/she/it has .... working	he/she/it has been ....

Negative

Full form	Short form
I/you/we/they have not been working	I/you/we/they .... working
he/she/it .... working	he/she/it hasn't been working

Questions

Have I/you/we/they been .... ? Has he/she/it .... working

Short answers

Yes, I/you/we/they .... Yes, he/she/it .... No, I/you/we/they .... No, he/she/it ....

Now check your answers in Lesson 6 STRUCTURES TO LEARN of the Students' Book.

2 Complete the chart.

noun	adjective
imagination	imaginative ....
patience	....
charm	....
determination	....
talent	....
energy	....
confidence	....
reliability	....
toughness	....

3 Fill in the chart. Use a dictionary if necessary.

job	place of work	equipment
teacher	school	books, blackboard
gardener	....	....
....	hospital	....
....	....	word processor, notebook
....	....	canvas, paints
chef	....	....
....	....	....
....	....	....
....	....	....

Think of three more jobs and complete the place of work and equipment columns.

4 Read the paragraphs and write questions. Use *How long?* and *How much/many?* and the present perfect simple or the present perfect continuous.

Dr Jenny Palmer has been working at St Thomas's hospital for . . . . She has been looking after the Children's Department for the last . . . . She has helped over . . . children to get better. She has only had . . . holiday in the last two years.

....

....

....

Tony French has been gardening for the last . . ., and has worked on . . . gardens in country houses. Since . . . he has been working at St Aldate's College and has planted over . . . new types of flowers in the gardens there.

....

....

....

Julie Dawn Rose has been writing for *The Independent* newspaper since . . . and has written over . . . articles. For the last . . . she has been doing research for an important article and has interviewed more than . . . people.

....

....

....

....

Now turn to page 74 and find the answers.

5 Write three sentences about yourself. Use the present perfect simple and the present perfect continuous.

....

....

....

6 Read the quotations about work. Decide if they are meant to be:

    a serious

OR b humorous/ironic

1 Work was like cats were supposed to be; if you disliked and feared it and tried to keep out of its way, it knew at once and sought you out . . .
Kingsley Amis

2 Anyone can do any amount of work provided it isn't the work he is supposed to be doing at that moment.
Robert Benchley

3 Work is much more fun than fun.
Noel Coward

4 Work expands so as to fill the time available for its completion.
C Northcote Parkinson

5 One of the symptoms of approaching nervous breakdown is the belief that one's work is terribly important. If I were a medical man, I should prescribe a holiday to any patient who considered his work important.
Bertrand Russell

6 I like work. It fascinates me. I can sit and look at it for hours. I love to keep it by me: the idea of getting rid of it nearly breaks my heart.
Jerome K Jerome

7 It is necessary to work, if not from inclination, at least from despair. Everything considered, work is less boring than amusing oneself.
Baudelaire

8 I work so hard to find out what I have to do, not what I like to do.
Mies Van der Rohe

9 To do nothing at all is the most difficult thing in the world, the most difficult and the most intellectual.
Oscar Wilde

10 Most of the world's troubles seem to come from people who are too busy. If only politicians and scientists were lazier, how much happier we should all be.
Evelyn Waugh

11 Our nature consists in motion; complete rest is death.
Pascal

12 When work is a pleasure, life is a joy! When work is a duty, life is slavery.
Maxim Gorky

Which quotations do you agree with?

'Apart from looking important, what other qualifications have you?'

7 Write a sentence describing your attitude to work.

....

....

❶ Write suitable responses to the following sentences.

1 His nose is red.
He's been sunbathing.......................................

2 She's got backache.

....

3 He's got food all over his face.

....

4 He looks as if he needs a break.

....

5 The car is full of groceries.

....

6 He's so dirty!

....

❷ Complete the sentences below with the *present perfect simple* or *continuous* form of the verb in brackets.

1 She looks as if she needs a holiday. She (work) .... very hard.

2 It's freezing cold tonight and I (stand) .... here for half an hour.

3 The marketing director is very experienced. He (work) .... for several major companies.

4 I (wait) .... all morning for the sales figures, and I (just get) .... them.

5 He (visit) .... our office in Belo Horizonte, so he (not be) .... here for the last two weeks.

6 She (read) .... the report, but she (not finish) .... it yet.

7 He (always work) .... hard, but recently he (leave) .... work even later than usual.

8 I (live) .... in London all my life, but in the last few years, I (travel) .... a lot.

❸ Write sentences saying what you've been doing:

1 today ....

....

2 this week ....

....

3 this month ....

....

4 this year ....

....

❹ Use your dictionary to find out about these words.

How many meanings do *insurance, sterling* have?
Which syllable is stressed in *geographical, institution*?
What parts of speech are *crash, influence*?

⑤ Make nouns from these verbs.

develop ....

invest ....

organise ....

recover ....

⑥ Read the passage and write a title for each paragraph.

FACTFILE New York City: population 7 million, incorporates five boroughs: Manhattan, Queen's, The Bronx, Brooklyn and Staten Island, total area 300 square miles; financial district centred on Wall Street.

1 ....

In the 1960s and 1970s New York faced a number of serious problems, such as a shortage of housing, increasing crime, and several financial crises which brought the city close to bankruptcy. Its recovery was only possible due to the assistance of the federal government, but this has meant that the city authorities have given up a certain amount of financial independence.

2 ....

Yet the city has still maintained its importance as a financial centre both for the USA and for the world. It is the world's largest capital market and its chief financial centre. It is the home of the New York Stock Exchange, which is a reference point for stock markets all over the world. The American Stock Exchange and numerous commodity exchanges, which trade in gold, silver, oil, cotton, cocoa and coffee, are also based in New York. It has about 25% of the international banking market. More than 3,800 major American corporations have their headquarters there. Six of the country's seven largest banks, with total assets of more than 200,000 million dollars, are based there, as are three of the largest life insurance corporations and a third of the country's largest retail firms.

3 ....

The New York shipping industry handles 15% of the country's overseas commerce, and has attracted to the city the leading marine insurance companies. The city is also important for its textile industry; from the nineteenth century's clothing workshops has come the modern fashion industry. Publishing, printing, food products and electrical equipment contribute to New York's industrial profile.

---

⑦ Answer the questions.

1 What do you think *bankruptcy* means?

....

....

2 What do you understand by *the city authorities have given up a certain amount of financial independence?*

....

....

3 Can you give examples of a *commodity*?

....

4 What industries and businesses make up the *industrial profile* of New York?

....

....

5 Can you give five examples of a *service industry*?

....

....

6 Would you describe New York's future as optimistic or worrying? Can you explain why?

....

....

⑧ Read the passage again.

Now turn to page 74.

---

4 ....

Above all, the service industries are of great importance. Business services, such as advertising, management, public relations, commercial research and equipment rental, can all be found in the city. Educational facilities are excellent; more than 75 colleges and universities make the city an outstanding centre for higher learning and scientific research. With the location in the city of all national television networks and many American newspapers, New York is the communications centre of the country.

5 ....

But at the beginning of the nineties, there have been signs of a new financial crisis, major causes of which are the weak property market and an insecure banking system. It remains to be seen if New York can recover from this threat to its financial future.

❶ Write the words and underline the stressed syllables.

/əsɜ:tɪv/ ....
/kənsɜ:n/ ....
/ɪmi:dɪət/ ....
/lɔɪə/ ....
/ɔ:dɪnri/ ....

Now check your answers in Lesson 8 WORDS TO REMEMBER of the Students' Book.

❷ Write five sentences describing what you need to learn English in the best conditions. Here are some ideas.

someone to talk to   lots of English books
background music   radio programmes in
a stay in an English-   English
   speaking country   a computer
a quite room   films in English
a penfriend   pop music

What I really need is someone to talk to
in English.
....
....
....
....
....
....
....
....
....

❸ Complete the sentences with *hardly ever* or *hardly any*.

1 Loud noise causes me .... stress.
2 We .... go to the cinema these days.
3 She .... got home before 8pm.
4 There's .... coffee in the pot.
5 She can't type, so she's .... good as a secretary.
6 He .... visited his mother.

❹ Rewrite the following sentences using *be (not) used to* + *-ing* / noun.

1 He usually takes country roads and not the motorway.
....
....

2 This is her first flight and she's very nervous.
....
....

3 He isn't worried about his lecture.
....

4 He has never been married and lives on his own.
....

5 She has always loved hot, spicy food.
....

6 He's very sensitive to what people think of him.
....
....

❺ Rewrite these sentences to show the difference in meaning.

1 I'm used to going to bed late.
  I used to go to bed late.
  I often ....
  I don't ....
  .... *any more.*

2 They used to work late.
  They're used to working late.
....
....
....

3 She used to travel abroad.
  She's used to travelling abroad.
....
....

6 Read HOW STRESS-RESISTANT ARE YOU? and add up your score.

HOW STRESS-RESISTANT ARE YOU?

No one can avoid stress altogether, but some people may be better equipped to handle stress than others; for example, those who are able to communicate openly with friends and family seem to deal well with stress. The quiz will give you an idea of how resistant you are to stress, or how vulnerable.

Rate each item on the test from 1 (almost always) to 5 (never), according to how the statement pertains to you. Mark each item, even if it does not apply to you (for instance, if you do not smoke, give yourself a 1, not a 0). Add up your score.

1 I eat at least one hot, balanced meal a day. ☐
2 I get seven or eight hours of sleep at least four nights a week. ☐
3 I give and receive affection regularly. ☐
4 I have at least one relative within 75 kilometres of home on whom I can rely. ☐
5 I exercise to the point of perspiration at least twice weekly. ☐
6 I limit myself to 10 cigarettes a day. ☐
7 I take fewer than five alcoholic drinks a week. ☐
8 I am the appropriate weight for my height and build. ☐
9 My income covers my basic expenses. ☐
10 I get strength from my religious beliefs. ☐
11 I regularly attend social activities. ☐
12 I have a network of close friends and acquaintances. ☐
13 I have one or more friends to confide in about personal matters. ☐
14 I am in good health (including eyesight, hearing, teeth). ☐
15 I am able to speak openly about my feelings when angry or worried. ☐
16 I discuss domestic problems – chores and money, for example – with the members of my household. ☐
17 I have fun at least once a week. ☐
18 I can organise my time effectively. ☐
19 I drink fewer than three cups of coffee (or other caffeine-rich beverages) a day. ☐
20 I take some quiet time for myself during the day. ☐

Total score _____

Now turn to page 74 to find out what your score means.

7 Think of someone you know well and add up their score. Use the questionnaire to help you write a description of their lifestyle.

My brother doesn't eat a balanced meal every day. Sometimes he only has a sandwich.

....
....
....
....

8 Look at the list of stressful jobs. Put them in order from 1 (most stressful) to 10 (least stressful).

accountant   astronaut   dentist   footballer
journalist   police officer   politician
racing car driver   teacher   TV presenter

Now write sentences describing what is stressful about the top three jobs on your list.

....
....
....
....

"The man is an absolute dynamo—works hard, plays hard, drinks hard and falls down hard."

❶ Complete the chart with these words. Some can go in both columns.

as soon as   when   after   before   until

clause (with a verb)	noun phrase

❷ Read the statements about social customs. Write T if they are correct for your country and correct them if they are wrong.

1 You always kiss hands when you greet or say goodbye to someone.

....

....

2 Women always go through the door before men.

....

....

3 Important guests must make a speech during a formal meal.

....

....

4 You say Sir or Madam to people you don't know.

....

....

5 Men take off their hats as soon as they go indoors.

....

....

6 No one has lunch before 2pm.

....

....

7 People often work on Sundays.

....

....

❸ Join the pairs of sentences, changing the verb form if necessary.

1 She'll find a job. Then she'll buy a new car.
She .... when ....

2 He'll reach an agreement with them. Then he'll call the office.
.... as soon as ....

3 We'll have lunch. Then we'll talk business.
.... before ....

4 I'll finish this letter. Then I'll go home.
.... after ....

5 We'll wait to hear from him before we do anything.
.... until ....

6 The Japanese greet each other. Then they exchange business cards.
.... as soon as ....

❹ Write a description of your daily routine. Use: *as soon as*, *until*, *when*, *before* and *after*.

....

....

....

....

....

....

....

....

❺ Explain the difference between the two words.

friend, acquaintance

....

....

refreshment, drinks

....

....

personal, professional

....

....

....

6 Read this passage with a dictionary.

The crucial card that tells you how low to bow
OUT OF JAPAN   Tim Jackson

1 TOKYO – What measures three and a half inches by two inches, is sold in boxes of 100 and can be found in the pockets of almost all adult Japanese males except policemen?

2 The answer, of course, is a business card. Going to a meeting in Japan without one is like going without a shoe: an eccentricity which a host will politely ignore, but which demands an explanation all the same. So important is the card, or *meishi*, that many Japanese businessmen will pretend not to notice a visitor while they fumble in their desks for one.

3 A book on doing business in Japan published recently by the Nissan Motor Company lists eight rules on how to give and receive cards. Have your cards ready at all time, to avoid that fumbling; hand them over with one hand, standing up, pronouncing your name clearly as you do so; and when you receive someone else's card, do not play about with it. Study it carefully, put it down in front of you, and 'refer to it from time to time to show polite interest in your new acquaintance's position and responsibilities'.

4 Cards were first used in Japan during the Edo period – from 1603 to the mid-nineteenth century – by government officials who had to deal with foreigners. Like umbrellas, however, they have become more widely used in Japan than in the West.

5 The technology transfer now seems to be working in reverse, as foreigners realise how convenient they are. At English dinner parties in Tokyo, no one wants to be the first to pull out a card; but let someone else make the *faux pas*,* and an avalanche of paper will follow.

6 For Japanese, however, *meishi* mean more than just convenience. They are a crucial clue to status. A glance at the visitor's business card tells a businessman how low to bow, and what degree of politeness to use in the highly hierarchic Japanese language.

**faux pas* socially embarrassing mistake

7 Read the passage again. In which paragraphs do you find information about . . .?

a the advantages of using business cards
b the way to present a business card
c the history of business cards
d the importance of the business card

You may find this information in more than one paragraph.

8 Write down who or what the words in italics refer to.

1 Going to a meeting in Japan without *one* . . .

....

2 . . . an eccentricity which a host will politely ignore, but *which* demands an explanation

....

3 . . . many Japanese businessmen will pretend not to notice a visitor while *they* fumble . . .

....

4 . . . hand them over with one hand, standing up, pronouncing your name clearly as you do *so*; . . .

....

5 *They* are a crucial clue to status.

....

9 Read the passage again and write down anything which you didn't know or which you find surprising.

....
....
....
....

① **Complete the sentences with question tags.**

1 You will call me, ...
2 He doesn't eat very much, ...
3 She's very kind, ...
4 He can't drive, ...
5 You like Chinese food, ...
6 She hasn't arrived yet, ...
7 They aren't coming, ...
8 He was a well-known footballer, ...
9 She got married in 1950, ...
10 He hadn't heard the phone, ...

② **Read the situations and write down what you might say to a friend. Use question tags to ask a real question or to show you expect agreement.**

1 It's raining very heavily.

....

2 You have both enjoyed a film on television.

....

3 You want to know if your friend will be on time.

....

4 You want to be sure your friend can speak French.

....

5 You think the traffic is very heavy today.

....

③ **Read the situations and make suitable responses. Use *must* or *can't*.**

1 The baby's crying, but she's just had dinner. (can't)

....

2 It's midnight but he's still at the office. (must)

....

3 She's in the plane looking very pale. (can't)

....

4 They're holding hands and smiling at each other. (must)

....

5 I've called her three times, but there's no answer. (can't)

....

④ The passage opposite is taken from an advertisement for the British Airports Authority but it gives information about gestures and body language. Read it and find gestures that you make. What different meanings do they have for other cultures?

⑤ **Answer the questions.**

1 *cast* means actors or performers. Find two other words which explain why the writer talks of a *cast of 36 million*?

....

2 Look for a word in the first paragraph which has a similar meaning to *rubbing shoulders* in paragraph 4.

....

3 If you make an *unwitting insult*, are you aware of it or not?

....

4 Is *making a pass at* someone likely to be trying to begin a romantic relationship or wiping something from your eye.

....

5 For the British waiter, would two fingers be an insult or a neutral gesture?

....

6 Is *cabbie* likely to be another word for *British person* or *taxi driver*?

....

7 If the cabbie's gesture is obscene to the Sardinian woman, what does *clonk* mean here?

....

8 If *the Heathrow ballet is never dull*, then *Eyes peeled* is likely to mean *Watch your body language carefully* or *Watch other people's body language carefully*?

....

Now turn to page 74 and check your answers.

WATCH YOUR B*O*DY LANGUAGE

I'm never bored at airports. Quite the reverse. I visit them like other people go to the ballet. To a Manwatcher, there's nothing more fascinating than observing citizens of different countries mingling and exchanging body signals.

And nowhere is the performance so enjoyable as at Heathrow, the world's top international airport.

Day and night they pour in, a cast of 36 million a year from every corner of the globe.

Where else but Heathrow could you hope to see Brazilians rubbing shoulders with Brahmins, Poles with Polynesians, Madagascans with Minnesotans and Neapolitans with Nepalese.

Each nationality has its own language of posture and gesture. But since these body-lingos* are often mutually incomprehensible, an innocent gesture made in an airport lounge may well be an unwitting insult.

Something in your eye? Think before you touch the lower lid. If a Saudi sees you, he'll think you're calling him stupid, but a South American señorita will think you're making a pass at her.

There is no greater insult you can offer a Greek than to thrust your palms towards his face. This gesture, called the *moutza*, is descended from the old Byzantine custom of smearing filth from the gutter in the faces of condemned criminals as they were led in chains through the city.

So vile is this insult that in Greece even the Churchillian Victory-V is taboo, as it looks like a half-*moutza*.

Thus the Cretan or Athenian traveller, ordering two teas in a Heathrow restaurant will carefully reverse his palm and give the waiter two fingers.

With 22,600 orders for cups of tea open to misinterpretation every day, the wonder is the place functions at all.

A Sardinian woman asks if it is easy to find a taxi at Heathrow. The answer she gets is a cheery thumbs up. (Very likely from one of the 900 cabbies who serve the airport on an average day.) Immediately she clonks the unfortunate man with her handbag for making such a devastatingly obscene suggestion. This is why, incidentally, it's inadvisable to hitch-hike in Sardinia.

Isn't there at least one truly international gesture? Don't bet on it.

A Japanese asks an American passenger whether Heathrow has a luggage trolley service. It has. And as it happens, this service is not only first class but FREE!

So the Yank replies with the famous 'A-OK' ring gesture. But to the Japanese this signifies money, and he concludes there is a large charge for the service.

Meanwhile a Tunisian on-looker thinks the American is telling the Japanese that he is a worthless rogue and he is going to kill him . . .

But even if you're never treated to such a choreography of misunderstandings, the Heathrow ballet is never dull.

Eyes peeled, next time you're there.

* body-lingos body languages

6 Read the passage again and write down information about:

Gestures and their different meanings

....

....

....

....

Heathrow airport

....

....

....

....

What is the most interesting piece of information in the passage for you?

1 Decide which lesson of Unit 2 in the Students' Book the following words come from.

application   bad luck   business card   candidate
confidence   discipline   entertain   face   gesture
handwriting   hospitality   institution   invest   lock
manners   meeting   memory   mishear   noise
patience   refreshment   shares   sterling
stressful   surgeon   talent   tension   trading
turnover   visit

  6 Just the job!
  7 Factfile: The City of London
  8 Stress – a human concern
  9 *Sir, you have just given me my card*
 10 What do you really mean?

2 Look at the words in exercise 1 again.

1 Which words contain a silent 'r'?

....

2 Which words contain /ʃ/?

....

3 Which words contain /z/?

....

3 Write these words in the correct column and underline the stressed syllables. Some words can go in more than one column.

assertive   confront   identity   imagination
influence   lock   recover   reduce   reliability
strength   visit

noun	verb	adjective

You can use a dictionary to check your answers.

Complete the chart with other parts of speech formed from each word.

4 Complete the sentences with the words in bold.

ability, quality
  1 He has the .... to turn everything to his advantage.
  2 The .... I appreciate most is patience.

colleague, candidate
  3 He was a .... for the job but he didn't get it.
  4 A .... is someone you work with.

save, invest
  5 If you .... your money in stocks and shares, you can earn a profit or lose your money.
  6 He decided to .... his money and put it in a bank account.

refreshment, hospitality
  7 Can I offer you some .... , a drink or something to eat, perhaps?
  8 Her .... was very generous and I felt completely at home.

fault, mistake
  9 The television didn't work because of an electrical ....
 10 He made a grammatical ....

5 Choose ten difficult words or phrases from exercises 1, 2, 3 and 4 and learn them.

Now turn to page 75.

6 Write simple definitions for these words or phrases.

1 unemployment benefit ....

....

2 stockbroker ....

....

3 stress ....

....

4 on time ....

....

5 lecture ....

....

7 Check how much English you know. Answer yes (✔), not sure (?) or no (X).

Can you . . .?

form the present perfect continuous tense ☐
use *hardly any*, *hardly ever* ☐
use question tags ☐

Do you know how to . . .?

ask and say how long with *since* and *for* ☐
ask and say how much and how many ☐
talk about personal requirements ☐
emphasise information ☐
describe a sequence of actions using *as* ☐
    soon as, *until*, *when*, *after* and *before*
describe impressions ☐
make deductions ☐

Do you know the difference between . . .?

the present perfect simple and the ☐
    present perfect continuous
for and *since* ☐
be used to + *-ing* / noun and *used to* + ☐
    infinitive

If you answered *no* to any questions, look at the STRUCTURES TO LEARN in Lessons 6–10 of your Students' Book. Write sentences using the structures.

....

....

....

....

If you answered *not sure* to any questions, write sentences using the structures.

....

....

....

....

Now look at the STRUCTURES TO LEARN in Lessons 6–10 of your Students' Book and check.

8 Think of someone you know well and write a few sentences about:

• their school life or professional career
• their particular abilities and qualities
• what they've been doing recently
• their personal requirements for a stressfree, relaxed life
• their daily routine

....

....

....

....

....

....

....

....

....

....

1 Combine words from box A with words from box B to make as many compound adjectives as possible. Some of the words in both boxes can be used more than once.

A	B
grey old	behaved
	minded haired
left short	off known
strong	sighted
warm	fashioned
world	tempered
well	famous handed

....

....

....

....

....

....

....

2 Rewrite the sentences using adjective + infinitive constructions.

1 You remembered my birthday. That was kind.

It was kind ....

....

2 He passed his exam. That was clever.

It was ....

....

3 I heard the good news. I was delighted.

I was ....

....

4 Children must be polite to their parents. It's essential.

....

....

5 I can't walk very far. It's difficult.

....

....

6 Most people buy a newspaper every day. It's usual.

....

....

7 I missed the party. I was disappointed.

....

....

8 He lost his temper. That was rude.

....

....

3 Write sentences describing things that happened or that you did when you were a child. Use the adjectives below and a suitable infinitive construction.

1 difficult

....

2 common

....

3 proud

....

4 sorry

....

5 good

....

6 stupid

....

....

4 Read the passage from *All Our Children* and decide which chapter it comes from.

1 New lives
2 Health
3 Talented children
4 Music makers
5 Belief

My name is Christine and I'm ten years old. I live in Brussels. My mother's Greek and my father's Northern Irish. I go to the European school which is a school with lots of language sections mixed – in fact all the languages of the European Community – English, French, German, Italian, Dutch and so on.

I was born in Greece, in Athens, and I lived there for about three years. Then I moved to England for a year. Nobody could understand Greek there – nobody we knew. So I went to playschool there and I had to learn English. When I was four we moved to Luxembourg. Then I spent afternoons at a day nursery where there were other Greek children. But at school in the morning I had to speak French, and on the streets and in shops. And I also learnt German at the school in Luxembourg as a second language, and that was about all until I was about six and a half. Then we moved to Brussels and I started going to the European school.

Sometimes I consider myself English – it depends what mood I'm in – sometimes Greek. At home I speak both English and Greek . . . it depends. When it's easier in English, I'll change to English. It's not that it's hard, that I can't speak Greek well, it's just that sometimes I can understand or speak better in English, sometimes in Greek. I don't really have a problem speaking English and Greek at home. But when my mum asks me a question, I've got

to answer 'yes' or 'no'. And in Greek 'yes' is *neh* but in English 'no' is *no*. So when I shout it out whatever I say my mum doesn't know whether I'm saying 'no' in English or 'yes' in Greek. So she gets confused and gets the wrong message.

I do my sums in English most times, but sometimes in Greek. I learnt my times table and everything in English. Sometimes I think in a different language, but mainly in English. English is really my first language. Greek, French and German are all second languages. I can speak a little bit of Italian and Dutch, too. I haven't picked up anything in Portuguese – too complicated I think. I can say a few words in Russian, though. My grandmother lived in Russia and so she sometimes speaks Russian at home. Like, for instance, *idi*, which means 'come here', or *dyengi*, which means money. But Greek is really my favourite language, because I speak it more than the others and I know it better, and that's the language I learnt first.

I think it's fun to learn lots of languages, but it depends on the teacher, really. I mean, when I once had a strict teacher I didn't like it. Eventually I would like to learn more than four languages – maybe Italian or Spanish or something like that. I'll get the chance to learn one more language when I'm in my seventh year at school, and then later on one more still. That will mean I'll be able to speak six languages altogether.

5 Write down facts about Christine, her family, her different homes and her education.

....

....

....

....

....

6 Write down Christine's opinions about the languages she speaks.

....

....

....

....

....

7 Write sentences comparing English with other languages you speak. Think about:

• how well you speak them
• how easy they are to learn
• how they sound

....

....

....

....

....

....

....

....

1 Look at the picture of the house and write six sentences saying where the following things are.

kitchen   bathroom   balcony   sitting room
boiler   telephone

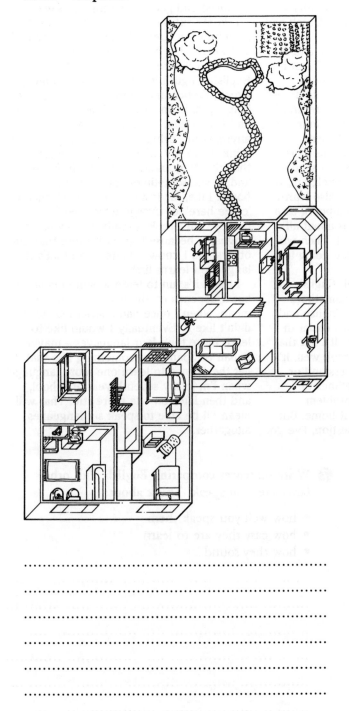

....

....

....

....

....

....

....

....

....

2 Compare the features of the house in the picture with those in your own home. Write sentences describing the differences. Use *whereas*.

It's got a large garden, whereas we have a small garden.

....

....

....

....

3 Complete the sentences with *who* or *that* if necessary. If they aren't necessary, write –.

The flat .... we bought is very small but it has a large balcony. The people .... sold it to us were an elderly couple .... wanted somewhere quieter. It's in a block .... was built about thirty years ago in a style .... is now quite old-fashioned. Fortunately it's not far from the friends .... we see most often. It's half an hour by bus to the company .... I work for. There's a street .... is only five minutes' walk away with plenty of shops.

4 Write answers to these questions.

1 How often do people move home in your country?

....

....

2 Do people in your country live in extended family groups?

....

....

3 Do most people in cities live in flats or houses?

....

....

4 How many rooms per family member do most people have in your country?

....

....

5 Do many young people own their own homes?

....

....

5 The passage opposite comes from a book called *A Year in Provence*. (Provence is a region in southern France.) Read it and decide if it comes from the beginning, the middle or the end of the book.

6 Choose the sentence which best describes what the book is likely to be about.

1 It is a description of the tourist attractions and facilities in southern France, especially for the visitor from England.
2 It describes the experiences of an English couple in their new home in Provence.
3 It is a guide to the architecture of Provence, dealing primarily in houses lived in by farmworkers and tourists.

7 Decide if the words in italics create a positive (+) or a negative (−) impression of the writer's feelings.

1 . . . two or three weeks of *true heat and sharp light.*
2 . . . during the *long grey winters and the damp green summers* . . .
3 . . . a colour somewhere between *pale honey and pale grey.*

8 Read the passage again and write down facts about the writer and the house.

....
....
....
....
....
....

Would you like to live in the house?

We had been here often before as tourists, desperate for our annual ration of two or three weeks of true heat and sharp light. Always when we left, with peeling noses and regret, we promised ourselves that one day we would live here. We had talked about it during the long grey winters and the damp green summers, looked with an addict's longing at photographs of village markets and vineyards, dreamed of being woken up by the sun slanting through the bedroom window. And now, somewhat to our surprise, we had done it. We had committed ourselves. We had bought a house, taken French lessons, said our goodbyes, shipped over our two dogs and become foreigners.

In the end, it had happened quickly – almost impulsively – because of the house. We saw it one afternoon and had mentally moved in by dinner.

It was set above the country road that runs between the two mediaeval villages of Ménerbes and Bonnieux, at the end of a dirt track through cherry trees and vines. It was a *mas*, or farmhouse, built from local stone which two hundred years of wind and sun had weathered to a colour somewhere between pale honey and pale grey. It had started life in the eighteenth century as one room and, in the haphazard manner of agricultural buildings, had spread to accommodate children, grandmothers, goats and farm implements until it had become an irregular three-storey house. Everything about it was solid. The spiral staircase which rose from the wine *cave* to the top floor was cut from massive slabs of stone. The walls, some of them a metre thick, were built to keep out the winds of the Mistral which, they say, can blow the ears off a donkey. Attached to the back of the house was an enclosed courtyard, and beyond that a bleached white stone swimming pool. There were three wells, there were established shade trees and slim green cypresses, hedges of rosemary, a giant almond tree. In the afternoon sun, with the wooden shutters half-closed like sleepy eyelids, it was irresistible.

1 Write these words in the correct column.

chest   dizziness   food poisoning   hips
injection   malaria   operation   pill   runny nose
stomach   temperature

part of body	illness	symptom	treatment

2 What parts of the body are affected by the following illnesses?

flu   ....

food poisoning ....

sunstroke   ....

appendicitis   ....

3 Complete the sentences with *both, both of, neither, neither of, nor.*

1 .... hospitals are equally good.

2 .... complaint is very serious.

3 .... the operation

.... the treatment will mean a
stay in hospital.

4 .... food poisoning and malaria
can sometimes be dangerous.

5 .... us have headaches, and
my wife has a runny nose as well.

6 .... us feels well and we

have .... got temperatures.

4 Complete these sentences describing cause and effect. Use *the* + comparative adjective.

1 The earlier I get up, ...
....

2 The later I go to bed, ...
....

3 The harder I work, ...
....

4 The more exercise I take, ...
....

5 The more English I learn, ...
....

6 The more I think about life, ...
....

5 Write three more sentences about yourself using *the* + comparative adjective.

....
....
....
....
....
....

6 You are going to read a passage called MY WEEK, which is written by a newly qualified doctor. Before you read it, predict which of the following words are likely to appear. Use your dictionary if necessary.

apartment   blood   casualty   consultant   drugs
emergency   gesture   patient   politician   round
sister   surgery   terrace   test   theatre   ward

Now read the passage and see if you were right.

7 Read the passage again and note down any impressions you form about:

- the doctor's hours of work
- her responsibilities
- her social life

....
....
....

My week

Rebecca Hodson sets out as a new doctor.

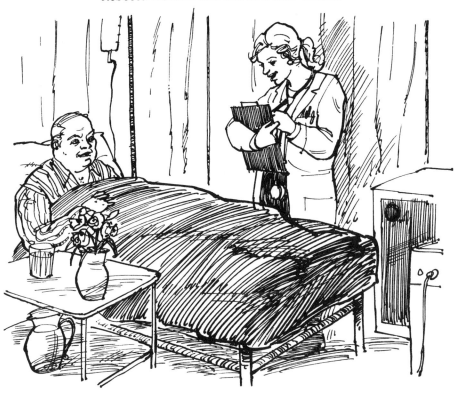

Thursday At 8.30am I start employment as a wage-earning junior doctor. After five years at medical school I and the other new house officers attend a two-hour introductory course to learn how to do the other 90 per cent of the job. The agenda is inspiring: Major Accidents are covered in 10 minutes. I am sure I can create one on the wards in much less time.

Friday I arrive on the ward at 7am, in good time to ensure that if the condition of any of my patients has deteriorated overnight I can find out about it from the doctor on call. There are blood results to check and samples to take. At 8.04 one consultant, one senior registrar, one ward sister, one house officer and two medical students begin the morning round.

From 9am on Friday until 9am on Monday I am on call. The on-call house surgeon looks after their own patients, those of their colleagues, and helps the on-call registrar to manage the surgical emergencies that arrive through casualty. For most of the day I see ward patients, inserting intravenous drips, prescribing drugs, following up test results and arranging scans.

At 7.15pm I go to the canteen for supper. Fifteen minutes later I am called to casualty to examine a patient who needs to go to theatre that evening. At 11.45pm I leave casualty to face an uncomfortable, but surprisingly undisturbed, first night in a hospital on-call room.

Saturday Ward round at 8am with the registrar and a very keen medical student, to catch up on the progress of patients admitted the day before. Later, I arrange an X-ray for a patient who might have a kidney stone.

During lunch I am bleeped by my registrar who is in casualty again. I am learning to eat quickly. At 1.30pm two patients with suspected appendicitis arrive. I sort out the paperwork and go to assist with surgery.

At 12.30am I leave casualty, having seen another patient who is to be admitted for observation.

Sunday I lie in until 9am, but then am called to see a patient with abdominal pain. I spend much of the day examining patients who are going to have surgery, with occasional excursions to casualty and the other wards. I see the last patient at 8pm and finish most of the work for that day by 11pm. I am called twice during the night, but only have to go to casualty once.

Monday 8am and I join the morning ward round, having told my opposite number about his patients' progress during the weekend.

At 1.30pm some patients arrive to sign their forms of consent for surgery before getting changed into their theatre gowns. The procedures are mainly simple removals of lumps and bumps which I mark with large circles using a waterproof pen.

At 5.10pm I ring my boyfriend to arrange supper and break the news that I need to spend our evening together in the supermarket, as I had cleared the food from my flat when I left on Friday morning. At 5.35pm I hand over to the new on-call house officer, turn off my bleeper and go home to refresh myself for the next day, when I am on call again.

8 **Which of these words would you use to describe the young doctor or her attitude to her new job?**

busy   dedicated   depressed   happy
hard-working   hungry   kind   overworked   tired

1 Write down two nouns which go with each adjective.

cheap ....

clean ....

decent ....

easy ....

free ....

poor ....

2 Use your dictionary to find out about these words.

1 How many meanings do *career*, *industry* have?
2 Which syllable is stressed in *conditions*, *revolve*?
3 What parts of speech are *benefit*, *total*?

3 Rewrite these sentences using the word in brackets.

1 In the 1920s many middle-class families didn't have much money, but they still employed servants. (although)

....

....

2 The houses they lived in were small, but there was usually a garden. (however)

....

....

3 Although it was expensive, many people wanted private education for their children. (but)

....

....

4 Although they had someone to look after the children, most middle-class women didn't have paid employment. (in spite of)

....

....

5 Although the economy was strong at the start of the decade, by 1929 it was very weak. (despite)

....

....

4 Write sentences about the five things which you think are most important for a good standard of living today.

....

....

....

....

5 Write sentences with *even*. Use the words in brackets.

1 Our four-year-old son Jack always gets up early. (at the weekend)

....

....

2 He has always liked books. (when he was too young to read)

....

....

3 He tries to make us read to him. (during meals)

....

4 He wants to go to school all the time. (on holiday)

....

5 He talks all the time. (when he's trying to go to sleep)

....

6 He doesn't like walking. (to the sweet shop)

....

....

6 Write surprising information about someone you know. Use *even*.

....

....

....

....

....

7 Read the passage and decide where these sentences go.

a But they could not earn enough, so they had to work long hours in the noisy mills.

b So they lived with their grandfather, Daniel.

c Sunday was the only day off work in which they could learn these things.

d Even the youngest, Sally, had to earn her keep.

e This had no fresh water and no lavatories.

8 Write a few sentences about a period in your country's history, perhaps ten years ago. Use the paragraph headings in the passage to help you.

....
....
....
....
....
....
....
....
....
....

1845: The Coggans

Hard times for the poor Coggan family meant a life in early Victorian England which was nearly all work and no play.

Who they were
The Coggan children were Hannah, Joseph, Roger and Sally. Their mother had died and their father had been sent to Australia for fighting to allow ordinary people a fair say.

Like their Uncle Gideon, they all had to work to eat. It was a hard life, but it was like that for many poor people in Britain.

Working and eating
Grandfather Daniel wove cloth by hand. But his old ways were not as fast as the new machines.

At first, to earn money, Hannah tried to be a maid in a rich household. Gideon and Roger helped some workers dig a tunnel for the new railway. They spent the money on potatoes, bread, a little meat, and sometimes a pie to cook in the local oven.

How they learned
Young Sally and Roger learned their letters and sums from the blacksmith. They were luckier than most grown-ups in England, nearly half of whom could not write their own names.

Later, when they lived in town, the children went to Sunday school. Here they were taught religion, but they also studied reading, writing and arithmetic.

Where they lived
The children lived in a cottage in the wild countryside. They were happier there than in the workhouse where, like many poor Victorian families, they had had to live when their father was in prison.

Later they moved to Bradley. Like many new towns, it had too many people. So they shared a dirty house in a slum yard. Pigs and rats lived in the yard with them.

Changes they saw
The year 1845 was a time of change. Everywhere there were machines that could quickly make many things which before had been made slowly by hand.

Roads were tarmacked, and the busy canal system was used less than the new railways. Goods could now move easily across the land and seas. With this 'Industrial Revolution' came other changes.

As more people were given the vote, slowly the rulers in Parliament learned to listen to what the people said.

1 **Look at the map and write sentences saying where these places are.**

Aberdeen   Birmingham   Chester   Durham
Exeter   Ffestiniog   Gloucester   Huddersfield

....

....

....

....

....

....

....

....

2 **Explain the difference between the two words.**

1 border, coast

....

....

2 lake, ocean

....

....

3 mountain, volcano

....

....

3 **Write sentences describing the least beautiful or interesting place you've ever visited. Think about its climate, vegetation, population, location and entertainment. If possible, try to include some of its advantages as well as its disadvantages.**

....

....

....

....

....

....

4 **Underline the correct answer.**

1 It's a quiet place with a little/little to do.
2 The town band plays a little/little music in the main square in summer, but that's all.
3 It's an ugly place but a few/few people come here because it's near the mountains.
4 There's often a little/little wind in the evenings, so take a pullover.
5 A few/Few hotels stay open in winter because there are no tourists.

5 **Join the sentences with *too* + adjective + *to* + infinitive, or *not* + adjective + *enough to* + infinitive.**

1 The sea is extremely cold. You can't go swimming.

....

2 It was very noisy. We didn't get much sleep.

....

....

3 She wasn't particularly hungry. She didn't have much lunch.

....

4 The fish wasn't very fresh. We couldn't eat it.

....

5 He's very fair. He mustn't spend much time in the sun.

....

....

6 Read REASONS TO BE CHEERFUL, which is taken from the travel section of *The Independent*. Which is the most surprising information?

REASONS TO BE CHEERFUL

Recently I asked: When you return home after a holiday abroad, is there anything that makes you feel glad about getting back to Britain?

My question was inspired by *Down and Out in Paris and London*, in which George Orwell reflects on the pleasures of Britain after travelling abroad: '. . . bathrooms, armchairs, mint sauce, new potatoes properly cooked, brown bread, marmalade, beer made with veritable hops . . .'

Letters have poured in from readers with their own lists of favourite things they miss when they are away. For those of you settling back to workaday life after a summer trip abroad, here are some reasons to be cheerful . . .

SYLVIA O'LEARY Norwich: English bacon; parks with grass that you are actually allowed to sit or lie on; red buses; paperboys; the milkman with the morning pint; pub lunches; double cream; granary bread; and – oh bliss – after the relentless exhausting heat of 'abroad', the refreshing cool English drizzle that meets us at the airport.

RACHEL IVES Oxford: The sight of a game of cricket; scrupulous politeness – people who apologise for bumping into you when it was your fault; bus drivers who stop when you hail them even though you're not standing at a bus stop; pick-your-own fruit farms; vegetarian food; the sheer joy of a hot day because they are so few and far between; ice-cream vans; manicured lawns and manageably sized

insects; traffic islands and driving on the left; instant coffee; Earl Grey tea and chocolate digestives; sarcasm.

KIRTI JOSHI, Leicester: Hot mango pickle; Radio 3 cricket commentary; Channel 4 news; clever adverts and *Coronation Street*; variety of English accents; cynicism and humour; musty second-hand bookshops; winding B-roads; live music.

MRS R HAIGH Louth: British twilight; unarmed policemen; raspberries, gooseberries, apples; proper bread; biscuits and cheese.

FRANCES TOMPKINS London SE10: Primroses; hawthorn flowers; children singing; swifts at twilight and a good cup of tea.

BEVERLY ORTON London NW6: Marmite; live broadcasts from the House of Commons; leafy parks in London; bacon sandwiches; our special humour; our marvellous theatre; Boots the Chemist; our gardens; churches . . . goodness knows why I'm always trying to leave this green and once pleasant land.

PAMELA JEFFREYS Muswell Hill, London: Cream teas; steak and kidney pie; gooseberries; broad beans; sausages and bacon; large flat mushrooms; potted shrimps; pork and egg pie; steamed syrup puddings; cottage gardens; stately homes; the National Trust; Ramblers Association; public libraries; non-vocational adult education classes and English newspapers.

7 Make a list of the features mentioned in the passage which you can find in your country.

....
....
....
....
....
....

8 Write a paragraph describing the REASONS TO BE CHEERFUL about your country.

....
....
....
....
....
....

1 Decide which lesson of Unit 3 in the Students' Book the following words come from.

angry apartment attic border bruise
coast conditions decent essential feed
fireplace glad heart industry injection
left-handed malaria middle-class mortgage
neighbour ocean operation pain radiator
relieved sandy socket stomach tropical
unspoilt well-behaved

11 All our children
12 Home life in the USA and China
13 Britain in view: the National Health Service
14 100 years ago
15 The city of the everlasting winter

2 Look at the words in exercise 1 again.

1 Which words contain double letters?

....

2 Which words contain a silent consonant?

....

3 Which words are both nouns and verbs?

....
....

Use your dictionary if necessary.

3 Write adjectives which mean the opposite of:

clean   ....

common   ....

easy   ....

expensive   ....

hard-working   ....

warm   ....

well-off   ....

4 Write nouns which go with the adjectives in exercise 3.

....
....
....
....
....
....
....
....

5 Combine words from box A with words from box B and write down as many combinations as possible.

A	B
coast door drain food fire front home ice time tax	bell cut door free line pipe poisoning place owner saving

....
....
....
....
....
....

6 Choose ten difficult words or phrases in exercises 1, 2, 3, 4 and 5 and learn them.

Now turn to page 75.

7 Check how much English you know. Answer yes (✔), not sure (?) or no (X).

Can you . . .?

form compound adjectives
use infinitive constructions
   after adjectives
use prepositions and adverbs of place
use defining relative clauses without
   who, which, that
use *both* and *neither*

Do you know how to . . .?

express contrast with *whereas*
talk about degree
describe change
talk about cause and effect with
   the + comparative adjective
express contrast with *but, although,
   however, in spite of, despite*
emphasise using *even*
say where places are
talk about quantity
talk about cause and effect with
   too + adjective *to* + infinitive and
   not + adjective + *enough to* +
   infinitive

Do you know the difference between . . .?

   a few and *few*
   a little and *little*

If you answered *no* to any questions, look at the STRUCTURES TO LEARN in Lessons 11–15 of your Students' Book. Write sentences using the structures.

....
....
....
....

If you answered *not sure* to any questions, write sentences using the structures.

....
....
....
....

Now look at the STRUCTURES TO LEARN in Lessons 11–15 of your Students' Book and check.

8 Write a few sentences about:

• childhood in your country
• a typical house in your country
• how people pay for the health service in your country
• the quality of life in your country 100 years ago
• an interesting place you have visited

....
....
....
....
....
....
....
....
....
....
....

9 Look at the STRUCTURES TO LEARN and the WORDS TO REMEMBER in Units 1–3 of your Students' Book. Choose the five structures and the ten words which are most useful to you and write them down.

....
....
....
....
....
....
....
....

1 Write the words in the correct column. Use a dictionary if necessary.

actor advertisement aisle audience box office
cast circle critic designer director
dressing room foyer leaflet musician
photograph playwright poster programme
review script seat stage stalls ticket

parts of theatre	people	publicity and print
....	....	....
....	....	....
....	....	....
....	....	....
....	....	....
....	....	....
....	....	....
....	....	....

2 Complete the sentences with (*to +*) the passive infinitive of the verbs in brackets.

1 I used .... to the theatre when I was a child. (take)

2 The lights should .... at the end of the show. (turn out)

3 Tickets can .... in advance. (buy)

4 Some actors want .... what to do. (tell)

5 He hoped .... a part in the play. (offer)

6 The costumes must .... by tonight. (finish)

7 The script needs .... (change)

8 Drinks will .... in the interval. (serve)

3 A conference is being organised for 11 September. Look at the organiser's notes.

April
Plan the day's events
Invite the speakers
Book the conference hall
Advertise the conference

June
Reserve accommodation for the speakers
Organise transport
Print the programmes
Send out the tickets

10 September
Arrange the seating
Check the microphones
Provide tea and coffee
Buy the flowers

It's now June. Write sentences saying what has been done, what is being done, and what has to be done.

1 Accommodation for the speakers ....

2 The seating ....

3 The programmes ....

4 The day's events ....

5 The speakers ....

6 Tea and coffee ....

7 Transport ....

8 The flowers ....

9 The conference hall ....

10 The microphones ....

11 The tickets ....

12 The conference ....

④ The extracts on the right are from different chapters of *Being an Actor* by Simon Callow. Read the extracts and decide which chapters they come from.

Getting the Job ☐   The Dress Rehearsal ☐
The First Night ☐   Unemployment Again ☐

⑤ Write down what the words in italics refer to.

1   . . . or if they do, *it*'ll be in quite the wrong place.

....

2   . . . so how *can* the audience?

....

3   . . . but you don't take the *one* offered to you . . .

....

4   . . . because *it* might seem unprofessional.

....

5   If you have a job a few weeks *hence* . . .

....

⑥ Which of the adjectives below would you use to describe how the actor feels?

anxious   bored   confident   depressed   excited gloomy   nervous   patient   relaxed   restless surprised   tense   uncomfortable

How does the actor feel . . .?

1 when he's not working ....

2 when he goes for an audition ....

3 during the dress rehearsal ....

4 on the first night ....

A The whole day, from the moment you get up to the moment you hit the sack, is like no other. If anything, it's like some peculiar birthday. Everybody is extremely nice to you. There will be telegrams and cards, possibly presents and flowers. Your dressing room begins to resemble a hospital ward or a funeral parlour. Whether the director has called you in or not, you're unlikely to be able to resist the magnetic pull of the theatre. You'll pick at your lunch. You'll drink many cups of black coffee.

B There will be a number of people in the audience, most of whom will have seen it before, when they didn't laugh. Now they won't laugh again. Those who haven't seen it before won't laugh either; or if they do, it'll be in quite the wrong place. The play will seem to last eight and a half hours. You will barely be thinking of your performance because you're haunted by the fact that the lighting plan appears to have been designed by Rembrandt. You can't see your fellow actors, so how can the audience? All in all, you just long for the whole thing to be over.

C Theatre auditions generally take place in the auditorium of a theatre other than the one in which the play will go on. The director, the assistant director, the casting agent, possibly the theatre's artistic director, probably the producer, are all lounging in the stalls with their feet on the back of the seat in front. There are twenty or thirty plastic cups with cigarette butts lying in an inch of coffee littering the aisles. The air is thick with smoke and raucous laughter. The director has been telling a joke. About the previous actor, you think darkly, and they'll have a little joke about you too when you've gone. People leap up to greet you, the casting director introduces you to everyone, you shake the director as firmly by the hand as you can without betraying your tension. Your voice is trembling oddly. You long for a cigarette, even though you don't smoke, but you don't take the one offered to you because it might seem unprofessional, and your mouth is already so dry that it's painful to swallow.

D 'You deserve a rest.' No. The only thing I deserve, I hope, is a job. If you have a job a few weeks hence, then a gap of a few weeks will be most welcome. But any time, any day not working and without the prospect of work, is dead time, grey time, anxious and haunted times. You could learn German, take driving lessons, night classes in the History of Art. No, you couldn't. Even if you've got any money, which is unlikely, it's impossible to settle to anything. There's something wrong, something missing.

1 Look at the picture and write sentences saying what needs doing to the property.

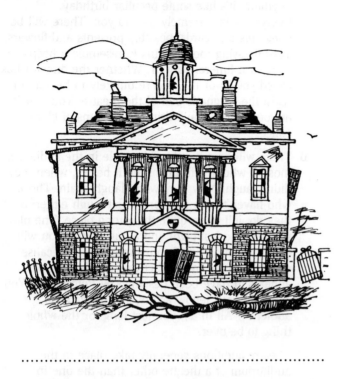

....
....
....
....
....
....
....
....
....
....

Now turn to page 75.

2 Write sentences saying what needs to be done to improve your town or city. Think about:

the transport system   streets   schools   houses
hospitals   sports facilities   safety

....
....
....
....
....
....
....

3 Write sentences saying who you would get to do these things for you.

1 install a shower

I'd get a plumber to install a ....
shower.

2 build a wardrobe

....

....

3 put in new sockets

....

....

4 arrange a holiday

....

....

5 replace your car battery

....

....

6 lend you some money

....

....

4 Complete the sentences with the correct form of the verbs in brackets.

1 We must get the windows ....
(clean)

2 I got someone .... the central heating.
(repair)

3 He has all his suits .... for
him. (make)

4 The baby's crying – I think she needs
.... (feed)

5 Could you get someone ....
the phone? (answer)

6 Is this shirt washable, or does it need
.... ? (dry-clean)

7 We need to have the bathroom
.... (redecorate)

8 I must get the car .... this
week. (service)

5 The extracts opposite are from *The History Man* by Malcolm Bradbury. They are not in the right order. First, read them and decide what the topic is.

....

Now put the extracts in chronological order.

1	2	3	4

6 Read the extracts again and answer the questions. Give your reasons.

1 Do you think Howard Kirk is a student or a teacher at the university?

....

2 Do you think Barbara Kirk feels depressed or happy?

....

3 Which of these adjectives do you think best describe Howard Kirk?

careful careless lazy busy tidy untidy organised disorganised

....

4 Who do you think Martin and Celia are?

....

7 Look again at extract D and write sentences saying what needs doing in preparation for the party.

....
....
....
....

Write about other things that need doing in preparation for a party.

....
....
....

A And so the Kirks get out, and go round to the back of the van, and unload what is there. They carry it, together, the bread, the cheese and the sausages, the glasses and the big red bottles in their cases, into the house, into the pine kitchen. They spread it on the table, an impressive array of commodities, ready and waiting for the party in the evening. 'I want you back by four, to help me with all this fun we're brewing,' says Barbara. 'Yes, I'll try,' says Howard. He looks at the wine; he goes out to the van. Then he gets in, and drives off, through the town, towards the university.

B After a while, Howard leaves the kitchen and begins to go round the house. He is a solemn party-giver, the creator of a serious social theatre. Now he goes about, putting out ashtrays and dishes, cushions and chairs. He moves furniture, to produce good conversation areas, open significant action spaces, create corners of privacy. The children run around with him. 'Who's coming, Howard?' asks Martin. 'A whole crowd of people,' says Howard. 'Who?' asks Martin. 'He doesn't know,' says Celia.

C 'When?' says Barbara. 'Soon,' says Howard. 'Are we free on the first day of term?' asks Barbara. It is improbable, but Howard turns the pages; there is the day, Monday 2 October, and the evening is a blank. It is almost an omen; and from his inside pocket Howard takes out, at once, his pen. He holds the diary open; he writes, in his neat little hand, as if writing the start of some new story, which in a sense is what it is, the word 'Party' in the small space of white on the crowded page.

D 'I said come back about four,' says Barbara, as Howard kisses her lightly on the cheek. She wipes the cheek with the back of her hand; she looks at him. 'I've had a busy day,' says Howard. 'I'm sure,' says Barbara. 'Don't tell me about it. It's clearly set you up in a big way, and I'm not interested in other people's happy times right now.' 'You're late, Howard,' says Celia, 'that was naughty.' 'Well,' says Barbara, 'there are the following things to do. Wipe the glasses. Open all the bottles of wine; there'll not be time for doing that later. I should pour out a few dozen glasses full. Put out ashtrays; I'm not having dirty rugs, and for some reason students have started throwing cigarette-ends on the floor.' 'They always did,' says Howard, 'we didn't care, once.' 'Well, we do now,' says Barbara. 'And then arrange the house, sociologically speaking, for all that interaction you're always talking about.'

1 Complete the chart and underline the stressed syllables.

noun	verb
appointment	....
argument	....
arrangement	....
complaint	....
control	....
decision	....
discipline	....
freedom	....

2 Robert's parents were quite strict when he was a teenager. Write sentences saying what they made him do, what they let him do, and what they didn't let him do.

1 'I had to eat things I didn't like.'

They made him eat things he didn't like.

2 'I wasn't allowed to have ice-cream.'

....

3 'I was allowed to choose my own clothes . . .'

....

4 '. . . but I wasn't allowed to wear jeans.'

....

5 'I couldn't go to the cinema with my friends.'

....

6 'I was allowed to watch television at weekends.'

....

7 'I could go to the park on my bike.'

....

8 'I had to go to bed very early.'

....

9 'I wasn't allowed to argue with them.'

....

3 Complete the sentences.

1 Customs officers sometimes make you ....

....

2 When driving, you aren't allowed to ....

....

3 If you travel abroad, you have to ....

....

4 People in prison are usually allowed to ....

....

5 If you haven't got a ticket, you can't ....

....

6 My parents used to let me ....

....

7 But they said I couldn't ....

....

8 I don't let people ....

....

4 Read the passage and decide where it comes from.

a publicity brochure ☐   a novel ☐
a biography ☐   a newspaper article ☐

5 Read the passage again and underline any information which you find surprising.

6 Write sentences about:

two things Summerhill pupils don't have to do

....

....

two things they're allowed to do

....

....

two things they're not allowed to do

....

....

7 Would you send your children to Summerhill? Say why or why not.

....

....

....

....

8 Write sentences describing some of the rules at your primary or secondary school. Think about these areas:

running shouting talking fighting subjects
games homework exams punctuality absence
personal stereos and radios eating drinking
smoking clothes hair make-up duties

....

....

....

....

....

Teach yourself freedom

Summerhill is a boarding school where children do not have to go to lessons and where a five-year-old has as much say as the head-teacher. It was founded in 1921 by A S Neill, whose ideals were that children should be happy and can be responsible for themselves. The school is an international community of children governed by children, with adult support only as they require it. 'Difficult' children can be successful at Summerhill because the problems they may have had in mainstream schools – not wanting to go to lessons, not fitting in, being bullied – are absent. One third of the children come from Japan, where there is an exceptionally disciplined system with heavy pressures to succeed.

A timetable is set after the 65 children pick what they want to do from a list of options. The youngest and the eldest go to the most lessons. Those between 10 and 12 go least. Occasionally, they will not learn to read and write until their teens. Lucille, 13, came to Summerhill when she was 10. 'As soon as you come here you think, OK, right, I don't have to go to lessons, and it's just a relief. Then after about three or four terms you start going again because you're totally and utterly bored walking around all day.' Those who attend lessons respond wholeheartedly.

GCSEs* are on offer, but not all take them. The Summerhill system looks to the eldest children for leadership and they have less time to study. Those who take examinations do well enough to continue in further education.

The community rules are set at weekly general meetings where every adult and child has an equal vote. The rules and the punishment for breaking them change constantly and currently run to four pages. Being noisy at bedtime can lose you a pudding, hitting someone can cost 10p, and climbing on school roofs can set you back £25.

A weekly tribunal hears serious charges. No one has to go but if a charge is being laid against you, it is in your interest to be there to defend yourself. Today, the chairman of the tribunal is Tegan Rannie, 17. 'Shut up, guys,' he yells, with instant effect at any group murmurings. No speaking or moving around the room is allowed without the chair's permission. Punishment for that can mean an instant 3p fine.

Two girls are sent to the back of all queues for a day for being noisy during the silence hour on Sunday morning. A boy and a girl are told to pay for new batteries for a computer game borrowed from a younger boy. A Japanese girl says she wants to change her name. Tegan advises her to bring it up at the next general meeting. An eight-year-old boy is repeatedly charged with offences. He is fined 50p for borrowing a bike without permission. He is banned from the older boys' rooms because he failed to leave when asked. He has to give a hug and a kiss to the school's principal, Zoe Redhead, daughter of A S Neill, for taking a ladder to climb into the stables with her four-year-old son.

Zoe Redhead was born and educated at Summerhill and her three older children have been, or are being, educated there. 'Even in the most modern, child-friendly school, children still have to sit still and be indoctrinated,' she says. 'People can become very self-motivated if you don't force them to do things.' She says that because Summerhill allows children to get rid of their repressions they end up as balanced members of the outside world. 'Summerhill doesn't produce any angry, rebellious souls. It produces rather boring and well-behaved citizens.'

*GCSE General Certificate of Secondary Education, usually taken at 16

1 You can do all these things with a ball. Match the words with the pictures.

bounce ☐   catch ☐   drop ☐   head ☐
hit ☐   kick ☐   miss ☐   serve ☐   throw ☐

2 Fill in the chart. Use a dictionary if necessary.

sport	place	equipment
tennis	....	....
....	pool	....
....	....	gloves
....	table	....
ice-hockey	....	....
....	....	ball, boots
....	....	clubs, ball
....	track	....
....	....	....
....	....	....
....	....	....

Think of three more sports and complete the place and equipment columns.

3 Complete the chart with 'people' nouns formed from the verbs. Underline the stressed syllables.

verb	noun	verb	noun
act	*actor*	perform	
box		play	
decorate		report	
direct		run	
edit		support	
inspect		swim	
instruct		train	
paint		translate	

4 Read the passage and identify the game.

.... is played .... two teams

.... a court .... a three-metre-

high basket .... each end. There are five

players .... each team and up to seven

substitutes. The aim .... the game is to

score points .... throwing the ball

.... the basket. Players run along,

bouncing the ball, and passing it ....

each other until one of them scores.

Now fill in the blanks with these prepositions.

at   between   by   in   into   of   on   to   with

5 Write a description of another game. Use the passage in exercise 4 to help you.

....

....

....

....

....

....

6 Rewrite these clauses using phrases with *during*.

1 while we were talking on the phone

during our phone conversation

2 while they were flying to Casablanca

....

3 while I was travelling to Oxford

....

4 while she was eating

....

5 while he was performing

....

7 Read BREAKING THE RULES and write the name of the sport above each extract. Choose from these sports:

basketball   boxing   football   ice-hockey
running   squash   swimming   table tennis
tennis   volleyball

Underline the words and phrases which helped you identify the sports.

8 Read the extracts again and answer the questions.

1 If players wore lead insoles in their boots, would it make the game faster or slower?

....

2 If players only had one serve, would their serves be more or less powerful?

....

3 If the square ring became a circle, would it make the sport safer or more dangerous?

....

4 To make scoring more difficult, would the basket be higher or lower?

....

9 Think of another idea for improving a sport. Describe the change you suggest and explain what effect it would have.

....

....

....

....

....

....

BREAKING THE RULES

Experts wrote to the *Observer* to suggest changes which would improve various sports . . .

1 ....

All professional players should be required to wear lead insoles in their boots, so that the game is reduced to a pace which requires the players – especially English players – to think more about their passing, and which allows their skills to be observed by onlookers.

2 ....

The serve used to be nothing more than a way of putting the ball into play. Now serves are the bazookas which capture championships such as the grass of Wimbledon or the rubberised cement at the US Open. The game would without doubt be more of a spectacle if the serve could be tamed.

Two suggested changes possess merit: one serve instead of two, encouraging players to emphasise accuracy instead of power; or a new service line forcing the server to stand a metre further back and offering the receiver precious extra time.

3 ....

Perhaps the most radical change would also be the most realistic – to change the traditional square ring into a circle, thus eliminating the corners in which fighters are all too frequently trapped. Referees often find it difficult to prise away an aggressor when he has his opponent pinned in a corner, sometimes with tragic results. A circular ring would make it easier to slide away from a barrage of punches and would also encourage more skilful use of the ropes as a tactical measure.

Heavier gloves and headguards are measures long debated but so far not adopted by the professionals. Perhaps it is time they were.

4 ....

It is the only sport I find boring – unutterably boring – and it's because scoring is so commonplace. The teams seem to be continually running backwards and forwards scoring hundreds of baskets, with the main scoring players tall enough to just plop the ball in the basket. Now, anything that happens easily isn't exciting. And in football it's the rarity of a goal – on average about two per match – that makes each goal such an important and exciting event.

So I'd like to see scoring made much more difficult. I would experiment with the height and placement of the basket so that the number of baskets scored in a game was reduced to about 30.

1 Complete the chart with adverbs of manner.

adjective	adverb
angry	....
beautiful	....
careful	....
casual	....
comfortable	....
good	....
guilty	....
noisy	....
proud	....
quiet	....
sensible	....
smart	....
truthful	....

2 Use suitable adverbs from the chart to complete these sentences.

1 When the woman was asked about the missing cash, she looked .... at the floor.
2 He always dresses .... in a suit and tie.
3 If you look .... , you'll see there's something wrong.
4 The police didn't believe the man although he answered their questions ....
5 She left the room .... and slammed the door.
6 I didn't do very .... in the exams.
7 The boy walked .... on to the platform to collect his prize.
8 The children are asleep so please talk ....

3 Underline the adverb phrases of place and circle the adverb phrases of time.

1 I'm going to the bank this morning.
2 Last year, we went to Jamaica for our holidays.
3 Meet me outside the theatre at 4.30.
4 In winter we often go to the mountains.
5 Then she drove over the bridge.
6 He goes running in the park after work.

4 Change the adverb phrases in exercise 3 and write your own sentences.

1 I'm going to the cinema this evening.
2 ....
   ....
3 ....
   ....
4 ....
   ....
5 ....
   ....
6 ....

5 Write polite requests.

1 You can't hear the radio properly.
   Would you please ....?
2 You want to borrow your friend's bike.
   Would you mind ....?
3 A friend comes to your home wearing dirty shoes.
   Do you think ....?
4 You give someone a pen and ask for their address.
   I wonder ....
5 You want your students' homework by Friday.
   Could you ....?

6 Read the first part of *A Fable*. What kind of story do you think it is?

a thriller ☐   a science fiction story ☐
a romantic story ☐   an adventure story ☐

7 Decide whether these statements are true (T) or false (F) and give evidence from the story.

1 The young man had a moustache.

....

2 He looked quite smart.

....

3 The people standing on the train didn't want to sit down.

....

4 The young man probably couldn't hear what the mother and daughter were saying.

....

5 He was probably shy or embarrassed when he sat down next to the girl.

....

8 What do you think the young man is going to do next?

a introduce himself to the girl
b ask where she's going
c make a comment about the weather
d pay her a compliment

Now turn to page 76 and find out if you were right.

9 Answer these questions from memory.

1 Why did the young man want to marry the girl?

....

....

....

2 The girl and her mother asked the young man several questions. What did they want to know?

....

....

....

10 How do you think the story ends?

Now turn to page 77 and find out if you were right.

A fable usually carries a message. What do you think is the message of this story?

A FABLE
by Robert Fox

The young man was clean shaven and neatly dressed. It was early Monday morning and he got on the subway. It was the first day of his first job and he was slightly nervous; he didn't know exactly what his job would be. Otherwise he felt fine. He loved everybody he saw. He loved everybody on the street and everybody disappearing into the subway, and he loved the world because it was a fine clear day and he was starting his first job.

Without kicking anybody, the young man was able to find a seat on the Manhattan-bound train. The car filled quickly and he looked up at the people standing over him envying his seat. Among them were a mother and daughter who were going shopping. The daughter was a beautiful girl with blond hair and soft-looking skin, and he was immediately attracted to her.

'He's staring at you,' the mother whispered to the daughter.

'Yes, Mother, I feel so uncomfortable. What shall I *do*?'

'He's in love with you.'

'In love with me? How can you tell?'

'Because I'm your mother.'

'But what shall I do?'

'Nothing. He'll try to talk to you. If he does, answer him. Be nice to him. He's only a boy.'

The train reached the business district and many people got off. The girl and her mother found seats opposite the young man. He continued to look at the girl who occasionally looked to see if he was looking at her.

The young man found a good pretext for standing in giving his seat to an elderly man. He stood over the girl and her mother. They whispered back and forth and looked up at him. At another stop the seat next to the girl was vacated, and the young man blushed but quickly took it.

'I knew it,' the mother said between her teeth. 'I knew, I *knew* it.'

The young man cleared his throat and tapped the girl. She jumped.

❶ Decide which lesson of Unit 4 in the Students'
Book the following words and phrases come from.

automatically broken cast casually costume
court cracked damaged freedom glance goal
hand over housework lay the table racket
rehearse repair scene score stalls strict
team teenage torn turn down

16 **Britain in view: The play's the thing**
17 **Give us a hand**
18 **Home rule – How liberal are you?**
19 **The most famous Number 10 in the world**
20 **True Tales of New York**

❷ Combine words from box A with words from box B
to make at least twenty-five compound nouns. Use
a dictionary to check whether the compound nouns
are one word, two words, or have a hyphen.

         A   **B**

home theatre window ice dry television tennis foot chess hair basket paint golf shoe

box mender hockey cleaner programme rink skates club cream set brush ball dresser work

....
....
....
....
....
....
....
....
....
....

❸ Complete these sentences with the words in bold.

rehearse, repeat
1 People often .... themselves when
they're talking.
2 The actors have to .... the play for
several weeks.

publish, publicise
3 The students put up posters to ....
the college party.
4 Writing a book is hard work, but finding
someone to .... it is even harder.

effective, efficient
5 Coloured lights can be very .... for
parties.
6 Normally my assistant is .... but
recently he's been forgetting things.

housework, homework
7 In most households, women do most of the
....
8 You should check your .... before
handing it in.

glance, look
9 .... closely at the picture and you'll
see someone you know.
10 I haven't read the report yet – I've only
managed to .... at it.

4 Write down three things you can:

turn off   *the radio* ....

take off   ....

take up   ....

put on   ....

put off   ....

hand out   ....

5 Write sentences using the verbs and nouns in exercise 4. Then rewrite your sentences using pronouns instead of nouns.

I turned off the radio. I turned ....

it off. ....

....

....

....

....

6 Check how much English you know. Answer yes (✔), not sure (?) or no (X).

Can you . . .?

form the passive infinitive

use the present continuous passive

use the present perfect passive

use causative constructions with
    have and *get*

use *make* and *let* + infinitive without *to*

form compound nouns

form nouns with the suffix: -*er*

use phrasal verbs

use adverbs of manner, place and time

Do you know how to . . .?

give opinions

express necessity

express obligation

express permission and prohibition

express instrument using *with*

make requests and complaints

apologise

Do you know when to use . . .?

make, do and *have*
during and *while*

If you answered *no* to any questions, look at the **STRUCTURES TO LEARN** in Lessons 16–20 of your Students' Book. Write sentences using the structures.

....

....

....

....

....

If you answered *not sure* to any questions, write sentences using the structures.

....

....

....

....

Now look at the **STRUCTURES TO LEARN** in Lessons 16–20 of your Students' Book and check.

7 Write a few sentences about:

- the best/worst play/film you have ever seen
- making preparations for a party in your home
- your opinion of how parents should bring up their children
- sports facilities in your town
- a situation in which someone made a complaint

....

....

....

....

....

....

....

....

....

....

....

....

....

....

❶ Rewrite the sentences using *will* or *won't*.

1 That's the last time I go by coach.

....

2 I'm sorry but I refuse to speak to her.

....

3 I promise to call when I get there.

....

4 Would you like me to do that for you?

....

5 Please come and stay with us.

....

6 Could you please close the window?

....

7 Let me carry your suitcase.

....

8 I'd like the roast lamb, please.

....

❷ Decide what you would say in these situations and write sentences. Use the function in brackets to help you.

1 A friend's radio is too loud. (request)

....

2 Your mother wants you to send a postcard when you're on holiday. (promise)

....

3 An elderly friend needs to go shopping and he hasn't got a car. (offer)

....

4 It's late and you're worried because your friend hasn't come home on time. (decision)

....

5 You'd like a friend to come to a football match with you. (invitation)

....

6 Your friend has just missed a bus. (prediction)

....

❸ Write down three things you can:

be aware of   ....

interrupt   ....

take part in   ....

❹ Use your dictionary to find out how many meanings the following words have. For each word, choose a meaning that is useful to you, and write a sentence to show how it is used.

complex

....

....

pause

....

....

signal

....

....

tense

....

....

trouble

....

....

❺ Write these words in the correct column.

attentive   formal   interrupt   mood   prediction
social   suggestion   threat

noun	verb	adjective

You can use a dictionary to check your answers.

Complete the chart with other parts of speech formed from each word.

6 Read the passage below and underline any sentences that contain information or ideas that are new to you.

7 Make notes on:

- how to start a conversation
- how to be a good listener
- how to take turns
- how to know when to end a conversation

....

....

....

....

Starting a conversation

Everyone finds it difficult to strike up conversations. The importance of doing so is obvious. To have relationships, you have to meet people and get to know them. To get to know them you have to talk to them. At some point there has to be an opening line, but how do you know what to say?

Conversations often begin when one person remarks 'Beautiful weather, isn't it?' or asks some other clichéd question. Conversation openers are rarely original – the anxiety of making the first approach is not conducive to creative thought – but this does not matter. What does matter is that these openers are recognised for what they really are – attempts at starting a conversation.

Once an opening line has been successfully delivered, a reply is needed. If the person who has been addressed wants a conversation, the reply must communicate this by being not too brief and by sounding enthusiastic enough.

Being a good listener

With the conversation opened, the next thing to do is to find out a few things about the other person – for example, by asking, 'Do you live around here?' People usually like talking about themselves. Encourage them by being a good listener. The best way of doing this is to give them a lot of feedback – lots of facial expression, nods and other body language signals and verbal signals like 'mm-hmmm' and 'yeah.'

People generally like talking to those who give a lot of feedback because they appear interested and interesting.

Taking your turn

We usually take it for granted that we will somehow effortlessly and efficiently interweave our speech with that of everyone else. However, this can be a great deal more difficult than it at first seems. Remember, those wishing to take the floor must begin immediately from where the previous speaker has left off. In a two-person conversation, the main importance of this is to avoid awkward pauses. In a conversation involving three or more people, you may not get to say your piece if you do not jump in promptly at the appropriate moment.

How can you tell when your turn has come? The simplest way is to be aware of pauses. Has the person finished speaking or are they simply stopping to think? Good listeners look ahead to predict and recognise their conversational partner's completion points.

Ending conversations

Just as it is important to know how to time an opening line, it is also vital to be aware when a conversation has reached its natural conclusion.

Keep an eye out for cues such as sighs, increasingly longer pauses, 'well . . .' and other open-ended verbal feedback as well as such body language as restlessness, less and less eye contact, and movement away. When you realise that a conversation is over, end it quickly but not too abruptly – even if both partners in a conversation know they have finished for the moment, you can still offend if you are too brusque when concluding. If the other person continues to cling to the last vestiges of talk, take the initiative and firmly close the conversation, keeping it as friendly as possible.

1 Write sentences saying what you predict or what has been arranged about the following. Use the structures in brackets.

1 the next Head of State of your country (be likely to)

....

2 the next election in your country (be due to)

....

3 the next government in your country (be expected to)

....

4 your next English class (present continuous)

....

5 an important arrangement for next week (be to)

....

6 your timetable for tomorrow (present simple)

....

2 Write sentences about the day's arrangements for Marie Clarke, a journalist. Use *when, as soon as* and *after.*

....

....

....

....

....

....

....

....

TO DO
Get to work 8.45am
Attend editorial meeting 9am
○ Do interview with Dr Frewin 10am
Write article 2pm
○ Edit final copy 4pm
Visit parents 6pm
○ Return home 7pm
Have dinner
Work on novel

3 Write sentences about your arrangements for tomorrow.

....

....

....

....

....

....

....

....

4 Match the words with the stress patterns.

arrangement assembly assistant candidate deputy election parliament prediction president senator

● ● ●   ● ● ●

....

....

....

....

⑤ Read A PRESIDENTIAL SYSTEM – THE USA with a dictionary. Underline anything that is similar to the system in your country.

⑥ Write down any vocabulary which you can use to describe the system of government in your country.

....

....

....

....

....

⑦ Write sentences describing the system of government in your country. Use phrases from the passage to help you.

In my country, the President is elected for seven years. ....

....

....

....

....

A Presidential System – the USA

Unlike the British system of government which developed through the centuries, the American system was carefully thought out in the 18th century.

In 1776, people living in Britain's American colonies rebelled against paying taxes to Britain. This led to the War of Independence and the defeat of the British in 1781. In 1783 the two countries signed a treaty recognising the United States of America as an independent nation.

The American Constitution

After gaining independence, the Americans wrote a constitution which was not completed until 1787. They created three branches of government: the President (the executive), Congress (the legislature) and the Supreme Court (the judiciary). One of the main aims was to prevent any one branch of government from having too much power.

The President

A President is elected for a four-year term and can serve a maximum of two four-year terms.

Role

• The President is head of the Executive Office which carries out government policy.
• The President can introduce Bills through a supporter in Congress. He is responsible for introducing the Bill concerning the annual budget.
• The President can veto Bills passed by Congress. However, a Bill can still become law if two-thirds of both Houses of Congress vote in its favour.
• The President manages foreign affairs and can make treaties subject to a two-thirds majority vote in the Senate.
• The President is Commander of the Armed Forces and can send troops abroad or use them to keep order at home.

Congress

Congress is made up of two Houses, the Senate (the Upper House) and the House of Representatives (the Lower House).

The Senate

Each state elects two representatives called Senators to the Senate. Senators are elected for six years but they do not all get elected at the same time.

One third of the total number is elected every second year to give continuity.

The House of Representatives

This consists of 435 Representatives who serve for two years. The number elected by each state is determined by the state's population.

Role of Congress

• Members from both Houses introduce and vote on new Bills.
• Congress can make amendments to the President's proposals.
• Each House checks any Bills passed by the other House.
• The President must get Senate approval before appointing certain senior staff such as the Secretaries (Ministers) heading the major departments.

Supreme Court

The Supreme Court consists of judges chosen by the President and approved by the Senate.

Role

• They can declare a law unconstitutional.
• The Court interprets the law, deciding what any controversial law means.

❶ Complete these sentences with the future continuous or the future perfect form of the verb in brackets.

1 I won't be here between three and four tomorrow. I .... (play) football.
2 Ring me on Friday, I .... (finish) the report by then.
3 We're very late, so when we get to the theatre, the play .... (start).
4 The big match is on TV tonight and I .... (watch) it.
5 This time tomorrow I .... (sit) in a plane on my way to Córdoba.
6 Next August we .... (live) in Oxford for four years.
7 I .... (go) shopping this afternoon. Can I get you anything?
8 Before the end of the day, I .... (spend) over £10 in all.

❷ Write sentences describing four things you'll be doing this time next week.

....
....
....
....
....
....

❸ Write sentences describing four things you'll have done by this time next week.

....
....
....
....
....
....

❹ Write these words in the correct column and circle the letters which match the sounds. Some words can go in more than one column.

cancer century communism decades emphasise financial heritage major nuclear pollution research resource

/k/	/s/	/z/

/dʒ/	/tʃ/	/ʃ/

❺ Write sentences which include the following adjectives.

cultural

....
....

economic

....
....

environmental

....
....

medical

....
....

nuclear

....
....

worldwide

....
....

6 Decide whether the following words will affect your life in the future. Write sentences explaining why or why not.

communism nationalism pollution research superpower

....

....

....

....

....

....

....

....

7 Read the short story opposite by Slawomir Mrozek and write a suitable title.

....

8 Have you ever decided to start a new life? Make a list of the things you would like to change in your life.

....

....

....

....

....

....

9 Make predictions about the things you wrote in exercise 8. Use the future continuous and the future perfect.

....

....

....

....

....

....

I decided to start a new life. My decision was firm and irrevocable. Only one question remained: 'From when?'

The answer was obvious: 'From tomorrow.'

When I woke up the next day I realised that it was today again, just as it had been yesterday. I couldn't start a new life today, having decided to do it from tomorrow.

'Not to worry,' I thought. 'Tomorrow will also be tomorrow.'

I went through the day in the usual way, at ease with my conscience, full of good intent and bracing hope.

However, tomorrow also turned out to be today, just as it had been yesterday and the day before.

'It's not my fault,' I thought, 'if some devil keeps changing tomorrow into today. My decision is faultless and irrevocable. Let's try again. Perhaps the devil will grow tired and tomorrow will be tomorrow at last.'

Alas, it was not. It was today again and again. In the end, I lost hope. 'Tomorrow will never come,' I thought. 'In that case, could one start a new life not from tomorrow but from today?'

One could not. The idea was absurd. If today had been recurring for a long time, there was nothing new about it, and no life starting today could be new either. A new life is a new life, and to be really and truly new, it had to start afresh, that is to say, from tomorrow.

I went to bed with a strong conviction that I would start a new life tomorrow.

After all, there is always a kind of tomorrow.

1 Match verbs from box A and particles from box B to make prepositional or phrasal-prepositional verbs. Use your dictionary if necessary.

A	B
ask get go care look	about after on at for on with up to

....

....

....

....

....

2 Choose five verbs you wrote in exercise 1 and write sentences showing what they mean.

....

....

....

....

....

3 Write down three things you can:

call off ....

fall in love with ....

feel sorry for ....

rely on ....

4 Think about four people you know. Describe their behaviour or characteristics. Use *can*.

David can be very charming...........................

....

....

....

5 Say where the following people might/could be and what they might/could be doing.

1 the head of state of your country

....

....

2 a member of your family

....

....

3 your favourite film star

....

....

4 your best friend

....

....

5 your favourite musician

....

....

6 Look at the people in the picture and say who and where they might be and what they might be doing.

....

....

....

....

....

....

7 Read the passage from *Hotel du Lac* with a dictionary and decide what type of novel it comes from.

science fiction ☐ a romantic story ☐ a detective story ☐ a western ☐

As the car rolled her on towards her destiny, she noted, with deep nostalgia, the Cypriot greengrocer emerging from the depths of his shop with a bucket of water; this was flung in a wide arc over the pavement, causing Edith to feel a shock of pleasure. She saw the hospital and the young men in white coats charging up the steps, and the adventure playground, and the day nursery, and the place that sold plants, and one or two pubs, and a rather nice dress shop. And then she saw the Registry Office and a small crowd chatting on the pavement in front of the entrance. Like a visitor from another planet, she saw her publisher and her agent and her poor father's crazy vegetarian cousin and several of her friends and quite a few neighbours. And she saw Penelope, animated, her red hat attracting the attention of one or two of the photographers, conversing with the best man and with Geoffrey. And then she saw, in a flash, but for all time, the totality of his mouse-like seemliness.

Leaning forward, in a condition of extreme calm, she said to the driver, 'Would you take me on a little further, please? I've changed my mind.'

'Certainly, madam,' he replied, thinking, from her modest demeanour, that she was one of the guests. 'Where would you like to go?'

'Perhaps round the park?' she suggested.

As the car proceeded smoothly past the Registry Office, Edith saw, as if in a still photograph, Penelope and Geoffrey, staring, their mouths open in horror. Then the scene became slightly more animated, as the crowd began to straggle down the steps, reminding her of a sequence in some early masterpiece of the cinema, now preserved as archive material. She felt like a spectator at some epic occurrence, was prepared for shots to ring out, fatalities to occur. But soon, amazingly soon, she had left them all behind, and as if to signal her escape the sun came out and blazed hectically, and with the full heat of a late false summer behind it, over Sloane Square. And then they were proceeding at a steady and stately pace through the park; Edith opened the window and breathed with ecstasy the fresher air, giving delighted attention to the little boys playing football, and the heavy girls thumping up and down on horseback, and the tourists peering at their maps and, presumably, asking the way to Harrods.

'Once more,' she begged.

8 Write down all the phrases used to describe Edith's feelings.

....

....

....

....

....

9 The novel was made into a film. Put brackets around anything which you think the film was unable to show.

10 Write words which you associate with:

science fiction ....

a romantic story ....

a detective story ....

a western ....

1 **Answer the following questions.**

What's your most amusing childhood memory?

....

....

....

Can you remember anything special about your
first years at school?

....

....

....

What memories do you have of a special place you
have visited?

....

....

....

What do you remember about your early
experiences of sport?

....

....

....

2 **Think about when you were younger. Write
sentences saying what you used to/would do.**

in the mornings

....

....

in the evenings

....

....

at weekends

....

....

on holiday

....

....

on your birthday

....

....

3 **Answer the questions about Susana. Use *was going
to* and the phrases in brackets.**

1 Did she go to university? (get a job)

No, ..., but
she got a job.

2 Did she get married to Juan Luis? (fall in love
with Pedro)

No, ... but

she ....

3 Did she stay in Fray Bentos? (move to
Montevideo)

No, ...

....

4 Did she go back to work? (have a baby)

No, ...

....

5 Did she travel round the world? (stayed in
Uruguay)

No, ...

....

6 Did she have her dream holiday in the Bahamas?
(go to Rio)

No, ...

....

7 Did she learn to play the piano? (learn to play
the guitar)

No, ...

....

8 Did she have English lessons? (decide to study
psychology)

No, ...

....

④ You are going to read about some people's
memories of transport. The speakers describe:

a an important event in space travel
b cycling along empty streets
c the London suburban railway in the 1920s
d a journey by public transport in the country
e the London Underground in September 1940

**Read the paragraphs and match them with the
speaker.**

1 One private bus made a point of never leaving anyone
behind, however full the bus. Sometimes there were many
more standing than sitting; or there would be four to a
seat, girls sitting in laps . . . At stops there always
seemed to be someone at the very back of the bus
wanting to get out. Amid groans from those already
squeezed as tight as could be in aisles and yells of
dismay as toes were unavoidably trodden on . . . those
nearer the exit piled out, sometimes into pouring rain . . .
or pitch dark, to let this one person out.

2 I can remember very clearly the journeys I made to and
from school because they were so tremendously exciting
. . . The excitement centred around my new tricycle. I
rode to school on it every day with my sister riding on
hers. No grown-ups came with us . . . All this, you must
realise, was in the good old days when the sight of a
motor car on the street was an event, and it was quite
safe for tiny children to go tricycling and whooping their
way to school in the centre of the highway.

3 In those days . . . the trains were steam ones, and there
was something awe-inspiring about the snorting, throbbing
engines which made the whole station shudder when they
drew in to the platform. Smoke puffed from the chimney,
and steam gushed from various points along the side of
the monster. Doors clanged, porters yelled, whistles blew,
flags waved – the din was tremendous.

4 People started to flock towards the tube. They wanted to
get underground. Thousands upon thousands of people . . .
pushed their way into Liverpool Street Station . . . Here
was a new life, a whole city under the world. We rode up
and down the escalators. The children of London were
adapting themselves to the times, inventing new games,
playing hopscotch . . . and I used to ride backwards and
forwards in the trains, to see the other stations of
underground people.

5 I remember the moon landing clearly because my father
woke me up in the middle of the night. He said that it
was an historic event and that I should watch it. Before I
went back to bed, I looked at the moon through my
bedroom window. It seemed odd to think that as I was
looking at it men were actually walking on its surface,
and that I had seen them on television. Since then I have
never been able to look at the moon in quite the same
way as before. It had lost its strangeness and mystery.

⑤ Decide which of the paragraphs describes what you
see in the picture.

⑥ Write down two things the speakers remember.
Use *remember* + noun/-ing/noun + -ing.

....

....

....

....

....

....

⑦ Write down two habitual and routine actions in
the past which the speakers describe.

....

....

....

....

....

....

....

1 Decide which lesson of Unit 5 in the Students'
Book the following words come from.

assembly   cancer   candidate   care about
childhood   communism   deputy   dialogue
engagement   event   experience   drug abuse
election   eye contact   feel sorry for   funfair
get cross with   holidays   memory   minister
monarch   mood   nationalism   nuclear   posture
promise   put up with   refusal   rely on
superpower   threat

**21 Making conversation: Do you need to change your
style?**
22 Britain in view: Time for a change?
23 Brave new world?
24 *A Room with a View*
25 Childhood memories

2 Complete the sentences with the words in bold.

event, experience
  1 I had never flown before. It was a completely
    new .... for me.
  2 Because of the rain, the
    .... had to be cancelled.

furious, cross
  3 I like her but she makes me a little bit
    .... sometimes.
  4 When she heard the news, she was absolutely
    ....

economic, economical
  5 It doesn't use much electricity so it's
    very ....
  6 The .... forecast for the
    next six months is not very good.

threat, warning
  7 Smoking is a serious ....
    to your health.
  8 The police let him go with a
    ....

relatives, parents
  9 Aunts, uncles and cousins are all
    ....
  10 Both my .... are still alive.

3 Combine words from box A with words from box B
and write down as many combinations as possible.

        A   B

A	B
eye civil cold life foreign personal nuclear prime science	affairs contact fiction expectancy minister freedom missile servant war

....
....
....
....
....
....
....
....

4 Write these words in the correct column and underline the stressed syllable.

angry cultural democracy economic
government hesitate insist pause political
rely tense vote

noun	verb	adjective

You can use a dictionary to check your answers.

Complete the chart with other parts of speech formed from each word.

5 Choose ten difficult words or phrases in exercises 1, 2, 3 and 4 and learn them.

Now turn to page 77.

6 Check how much English you know. Answer yes (✓), not sure (?) or no (X).

Can you . . .?

use *will* and *won't*
use future time clauses
form the future continuous tense
form the future perfect tense
use prepositional and phrasal-
  prepositional verbs
use *remember* + noun/ + *ing*/ +
  noun + *-ing*

Do you know how to . . .?

talk about future arrangements
  and predictions
describe a sequence of actions
talk about typical behaviour
  and characteristics
speculate
talk about the future in the past

Do you know the difference between . . .?

the future continuous and
  the future perfect
used to + infinitive and
  would + infinitive

If you answered *no* to any questions, look at the STRUCTURES TO LEARN in Lessons 21–25 of your Students' Book. Write sentences using the structures.

....

....

....

....

If you answered *not sure* to any questions, write sentences using the structures.

....

....

....

....

Now look at the STRUCTURES TO LEARN in Lessons 21–25 of your Students' Book and check.

7 Write a few sentences about:

* how easily you start conversations with people you don't know
* your plans for when you've finished this Workbook lesson
* someone you admire
* someone important from your past life

....

....

....

....

....

....

....

....

....

....

....

....

....

....

1 **Read the passage and decide where these words and phrases should go.**

a and turn b of drums c flowers d or lion
e dark and f of the celebrations g performed

On New Year's Day the festival moves into the streets. People wear beautiful costumes, and there are parades with flags, and fireworks. The most exciting event is a dance with a brightly-coloured model of a dragon. This gigantic animal weaves its way through the streets to the music, and seems to come alive when the dancers twist. Towards the end, the streets are hung with lanterns to welcome the longer warmer days after the cold of winter.

Now check your answers in the passage in Lesson 26 of the Students' Book.

2 **Many English words sound the same although they are spelt differently. These words are called homophones. For example, *here* and *hear* are homophones because they are both pronounced /hɪə/.**

The homophones for the words below are in the passage above. What are they?

weigh .... knew ....

where .... threw ....

their ....

Now complete the sentences below with the correct homophones.

/flaʊə/
1 Bread is made with .... and water.
2 The dancer wore a .... in her hair.

/wiːk/
3 He's still rather .... from his illness.
4 Let's have dinner sometime this ....

/pɑːst/
5 Go .... the bank and turn right.
6 I hope I've .... the test.

/miːt/
7 Did you .... anyone interesting at the party
8 Vegetarians don't eat ....

/tuː/
9 Could we have .... coffees, please?
10 I'd like a sandwich ....

3 **Read the jokes and riddles and match the questions with the answers.**

1 Why do police officers need to be strong?
2 Why did the man take a pencil to bed?
3 Why wasn't Cinderella any good at football?
4 Why is an island like the letter T?
5 Why did the man take a ruler to bed?
6 Why do artists never need to be short of money?
7 Why is six afraid of seven?
8 Why did the man sleep on the edge of the bed?

a Because it's in the middle of water.
b Because seven eight nine.
c So that he could drop off easily.
d In order to draw the curtains.
e Because they can always draw cheques.
f So that they can hold up the traffic.
g Because her coach was a pumpkin.
h To see how long he slept.

4 **Complete these sentences.**

1 I went to the bank in order to ....
....
2 People learn foreign languages so that ....
....
3 Florida is a popular holiday resort because ....
....
4 Since Murmansk is north of the Arctic Circle,
....
5 You should take a map in order not to ....
....

⑤ Join the pairs of sentences. You will sometimes need to change the order.

1 We wanted to get good seats. We booked tickets early.

....

in order to ....

2 She sat by the window. She wanted to enjoy the scenery.

....

so that ....

3 The flight is very short. So you don't get a meal on the plane.

As ....

....

4 You mustn't forget anything. You'd better make a list.

....

in order not to ....

5 Carnival starts tomorrow. That's why all the hotels are full.

....

because ....

⑥ Read THE DATING GAME and underline anything you didn't know or find surprising.

⑦ Complete these sentences.

1 Since the Mayas thought the extra five days were unlucky, ...

2 Julius Caesar introduced the leap year in order to ....

3 As the Julian year was 11 minutes and 14 seconds too long, ...

....

4 Pope Gregory dropped ten days from 1582 in order to ....

5 1900 was not a leap year because ....

....

6 People born on 29 February face jokes about their age because ....

....

The Dating Game

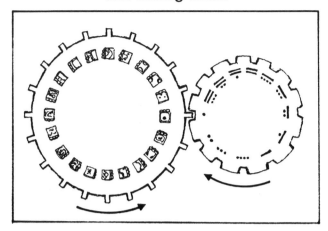

The earliest known date is 4236BC, when the Egyptians first established a solar calendar. They decided that there were 365 days in the year, based on the earth's orbit of the sun, and they divided their year into twelve months of thirty days. The five days left at the end of each year were celebrated as feast days. In Central America, the ancient Mayan civilisation also worked out the length of the solar year. They had eighteen months of twenty days each; most people stayed at home during the extra five days because they were considered to be unlucky and dangerous.

In 42BC Julius Caesar established the Julian calendar, which was based on the average solar year of 365¼ days. Caesar ordained that every fourth year should be a leap year of 366 days to allow for the odd quarter day. But the Julian calculation of 365¼ days to a year was 11 minutes and 14 seconds too long, so the calendar gradually fell out of step with the seasons.

In 1582 Pope Gregory XIII, with the help of astronomers, recommended changes in order to correct the calendar. By now, the Julian calendar was ten days 'slow', so he dropped ten days from 1582: the day after 4 October became 15 October. And under the Gregorian system, every four years is a leap year with an extra day at the end of February except at the end of the century; only century years that can be evenly divided by 400 are leap years, for example, 1600 and 2000. Women traditionally make proposals of marriage on February 29, and people born on that day face jokes about their age all their lives.

Although Jews and Muslims still have their own calendars for religious matters, the Gregorian calendar is now accepted by most countries of the world and used for international dealings. But the Gregorian calendar is still not absolutely correct and it will be out of step by one day when we reach the year 4905.

① Write the words that match these definitions in the first column of the chart below.

1 a scientist who studies the stars and planets
2 someone who studies ancient civilisations by examining their buildings and tools etc
3 a scientist who does research in chemistry
4 a scientist who studies plants
5 a scientist who studies living things
6 a person who forecasts the future through horoscopes

	person	subject	adjective
1	astronomer	astronomy	astronomical
2			
3			
4			
5			
6			

Now complete the chart with the help of your dictionary. Underline the stressed syllables.

② Write down nouns which go with these adjectives.

ancient   ....

complicated   ....

concrete   ....

congested   ....

fake   ....

religious   ....

③ Complete the sentences with *in*, *that* or –.

1 Do you believe .... the world was made in seven days?
2 When I was young, I used to believe .... Martians.
3 Many people believe .... life after death.
4 You shouldn't believe .... everything you read in the papers.
5 The man's story was so convincing that the police believed .... it.
6 She can't believe .... she's passed the exam.
7 I believe .... equal rights for men and women.
8 She said she was 16, but we didn't believe .... her.

④ Complete the sentences with *such*, *such a/an*, or *so*.

1 The story was .... ridiculous that nobody believed it.
2 The election result was .... good news that we all decided to celebrate.
3 He was .... tired that he fell asleep during the lecture.
4 It was .... interesting play that I saw it twice.
5 They are .... complicated instructions that no one can understand them.
6 She walked .... fast that the children couldn't keep up.
7 The mouse gave me .... shock that I screamed.
8 It was .... cold weather that the river froze.

⑤ Use the words below to write sentences expressing result with *such/so . . . that*. Don't change the order of the words.

1 film – sad – cry
The film was so sad that it made me cry.

2 popular – restaurant – always full

....

....

3 unexpected – information – surprised

....

....

4 building – old – dangerous

....

....

5 exercise – easy – five minutes

....

....

6 naughty – children – difficult to look after

....

....

6 Read the passage opposite and choose the best title.

BIG BEN FOR SALE
MONUMENTAL FRAUD
THE DISAPPOINTED TOURIST
LONDON BELONGS TO ME

7 Decide where these phrases can go in the passage.

a trying to sell the Statue of Liberty for another $100,000
b to meet soaring debts
c to 'agree the deal with his superiors'

8 Read the passage again and find:

1 a noun meaning *brilliant idea* ....

2 a verb meaning *noticed* ....

3 two separate adverbs meaning *in the end*

....

4 a verb meaning *agreed* ....

5 three adverbs or phrases meaning *immediately*

....

6 a verb meaning *take apart* ....

9 Write down what the words in *italics* refer to.

1 Introducing *himself* . . .

....

2 . . . Britain was having to sell *them* off.

....

3 The American begged *him* to sell the square to *him*.

....

4 The delighted tourist wrote *one* at once.

....

10 Choose the best definition of *fraud*:

a stealing money from people
b making money by deceiving or tricking people
c selling stolen property

Write down words for other types of crime. Use your dictionary to help you.

....

....

....

Arthur Furguson made money by selling things which weren't even his in the first place.

One morning in 1923, he spotted a rich American in Trafalgar Square and had a brainwave.

Introducing himself as the official guide to the square, Furguson explained all about Nelson's Column, the lions and the fountains – and just happened to mention what a shame it was that Britain was having to sell them off.

The American asked the price. '£6,000 to the right buyer,' replied Furguson, adding that, as guide, he had been entrusted with the job of making the sale.

The American begged him to sell the square to him. Finally, Furguson consented and went off. On his return, he announced that Britain was prepared to accept a cheque on the spot.

The delighted tourist wrote one at once. Furguson gave him a receipt – and even the name and address of a firm who would dismantle the square ready for shipping – and promptly marched off to cash the cheque.

Later that summer, Furguson went on to sell Big Ben for £1,000 and accept a down payment of £2,000 on Buckingham Palace.

In 1925, he went to Washington DC, where he leased the White House to a cattle-rancher for 99 years at $100,000 p.a. – with the first year payable in advance.

This type of business deal has a special name, of course: fraud. Furguson was eventually caught and was given five years in prison.

1 Match the words with the stress patterns.

agency completely decision difficult enemy
horrified proposal relation reluctant salary
secretly successful

● • •   • ● •

....
....
....
....
....
....

2 Write two homophones that match each of the sounds. For example: /si:/ = sea, see.

1 /fɔ:/ ....

2 /auə/ ....

3 /sɔ:/ ....

4 /sʌm/ ....

5 /raɪt/ ....

6 wʊd/ ....

3 Write down two nouns which go with each adjective.

empty   ....

clumsy   ....

stony   ....

cunning ....

unfortunate ....

4 Write down two adjectives which go with each noun.

friend   ....

enemy   ....

leader   ....

bargain ....

5 John is rather unusual. What would you have done instead?

1 John visited Alaska for his holidays.
I wouldn't have visited Alaska.
I'd have gone to

2 He took his swimming trunks and a sun hat.
....
....

3 He travelled from New York to Anchorage on a motorbike.
....
....

4 He slept in a tent.
....
....

5 He tried to shake hands with a polar bear.
....
....

6 Rewrite the sentences using third conditional constructions.

1 Lucy didn't have enough money so she didn't buy the watch.
If Lucy had had enough money, she'd
have bought the watch.

2 Bill opened the letter because he thought it was for him.
....
....

3 Since Pam had forgotten her glasses, she didn't enjoy the play.
....
....

4 Dave didn't hear his flight call so he missed the plane.
....
....

5 Sam and Toni didn't come to the party because they couldn't find a baby-sitter.
....
....

7 The extract opposite is from *I Am Right – You Are Wrong* by Edward de Bono. Read it and then choose the sentence which best describes what the book is likely to be about.

a It is a practical self-help guide on how to save time and organise your life more efficiently, whether at home, in the office, or on the golf course.

b It is a textbook for surgeons which describes the workings of the human brain in biological and medical terms, and gives details of scientific research.

c It argues that perception, rather than traditional logic, is the key to more constructive thinking and problem solving.

8 Answer the questions.

1 What do you think the young man's *standard eleven items of clothing* were?

....
....
....

2 If your brain worked like a traditional computer, how long would it take you to get dressed?

....

3 De Bono gives several examples of *routine patterns*. Write down as many as you can.

....
....
....
....
....
....

4 Give an example of a situation when you can't rely on *routine patterns of meaning*.

....
....

5 Why we should be grateful that the brain sets up sequence patterns?

....
....

Could you afford to spend 45 hours getting dressed every morning? If not, be grateful that the brain sets up sequence patterns.

One day a young man decided to figure out in how many ways he could get dressed using his standard 11 items of clothing. He set up his personal computer to do the work for him. The computer worked for 45 hours non-stop to show that out of the 39 million possible ways of putting on 11 items of clothing only about 5000 were possible (you could not put your shoes on before your socks, for example). The figure of 39 million is easily obtained because you have 11 choices of the first item and then for each of these 10 choices of the next, so you multiply $11 \times 10 \times 9 \times 8 \times 7 \times 6 \times 5 \times 4 \times 3 \times 2$.

The point is that if our brains worked like traditional computers it would take us about two days to get dressed, a week to make breakfast and a week to get to work. You would have to figure out how to hold a glass each time you picked one up, how to fill it and how to drink from it.

But we get dressed in normal time and drink normally from a glass because the brain behaves as a self-organising system that sets up routine patterns. Once the patterns are established, we just use them. We should be immensely grateful for such patterning behaviour because without it life would be utterly impossible.

If the brain were not a pattern-making system we would not be able to read, write or talk. Every activity, like getting dressed in the morning, would be a major time-consuming task. Sport would be impossible – for example, a golfer would have consciously to direct every part of every swing. Consider the millions of people who drive along the roads every day using patterns of perception and reaction and only occasionally having to work things out. There are routine patterns of action like driving or playing golf. There are routine patterns of perception, which is why we can recognise knives, forks and people. There are routine patterns of meaning, which is why we can listen and read and communicate.

1 Combine words from box A with words from box B and write down as many compound nouns as possible.

A

continuous

correspondence

vocational

private

state

physical

final

social

B

education

training   services

examination

assessment

science

course

school

....

....

....

....

....

....

....

....

....

....

....

2 Write a word map using these words.

certificate   college   degree   diploma   economics
philosophy   pupil   school   student   teacher
university   geography

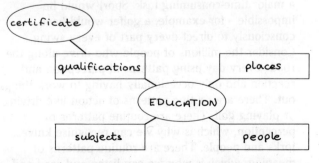

Add as many words as you can to your word map.

3 Complete the sentences with the correct form of the verbs in brackets.

1 I wish I .... more time to read these days. (have)

2 If only you .... yesterday when there were still some tickets left. (phone)

3 I wish I .... sing in tune. (can)

4 Don't you wish you .... to drive several years ago? (learn)

5 If only I .... go to work tomorrow. (not have to)

6 I wish I .... taller. (be)

7 I wish we .... an argument last night. (not have)

8 I've no idea what the answer is – I wish I .... (know)

4 Write sentences beginning *I wish . . . would . . .*

1 The people next door are having a party and the music is very loud.

....

....

2 You're trying to take notes but the teacher is talking too fast.

....

3 You're waiting to go out with a friend but she's taking a long time to get ready.

....

4 You like getting letters from a friend but he hardly ever writes to you.

....

....

5 You are annoyed because you feel your parents treat you like a child.

....

....

⑤ Write sentences about some of your wishes for change in the present. Think about:

your appearance   your abilities   your school/job
your home   your town   the government

....

....

....

....

....

....

⑥ Read I WISH I'D KNOWN . . . and decide whether Sue Lawley enjoyed her years at university. In which paragraph does she make her feelings clear?

⑦ In which paragraph does Sue refer to . . .?

a student politics
b love affairs
c useful professional connections
d the way she spoke
e the subject she studied

⑧ Write four more sentences saying what Sue regrets.

She wishes she hadn't given up history.

....

....

....

....

⑨ Think of times when you wish you'd known what you know now. Write sentences saying what you wish you'd known, and why.

....

....

....

....

....

....

I WISH I'D KNOWN . . .

Sue Lawley is a well-known TV presenter. She was a student of modern languages at Bristol University from 1964–67.

1 'I wish I'd known that modern languages wouldn't be desperately necessary in my career and that in fact history would have been far more useful. It gets life in context and because I gave up history at school, everything that happened after 1701 is self-taught or non-existent.

2 'I wish I'd known that I was going to be at university at such a fascinating time. Not just because of the Beatles and the Rolling Stones, but between 1964 and 1967 the whole student-power thing was brewing. I was president of the union, and on looking back I suppose I could have taken a more active part. A lot of what the students were worried about had some justifiable foundation. I think I was a little conservative and proper about it all.

3 'I wish I'd known before I went that pronouncing bath to rhyme with mat didn't really matter. I worried a lot about my accent and flattened it out no end. I don't regret that because it's been worthwhile professionally. But I regret that my accent made me feel inferior. That was silly.

4 'I wish I'd known that many of the unlikeliest people I would meet there would echo through the rest of my life as TV producers, MPs, journalists or actors. I would have taken more notice of them at the time.

5 'I wish I'd known it was to be one of the best periods of my life. I was surrounded by so many friends and had so many opportunities to enjoy total freedom without any real responsibility. It was wonderful and I envy people who are there now.

6 'My last and silly thought was: I wish I'd known that summers would never be so long, hot and romantic again.'

1 All these irregular verbs appear in YOU AND I ARE ABOUT TO DIE. Complete the chart.

infinitive	past simple	past participle
....	began	....
....	bet	....
....	....	bitten
....	....	blown
break	....	....
....	built	....
....	....	burned
fall	....	....
....	felt	....
....	found	....
....	gave	....
hit	....	....
....	held	....
know	....	....
....	....	left
....	lost	....
....	misunderstood	....
....	said	....
....	shook	....
show	....	....
....	shut	....
....	spilled	....
....	....	stolen
take	....	....
tell	....	....
....	thought	....
win	....	....

Now check your answers in the list of irregular verbs on pages 113 and 114 of the Students' Book.

2 Write sentences in response to the situations. Use must have or can't have.

1 Tom didn't come to the meeting this morning.

....

2 The audience didn't laugh once during the play.

....

3 Sue's just come back from Tunisia, but she's not at all brown.

....

4 David stayed up working all last night.

....

5 I gave Jane directions to the station – where is she?

....

6 Paul failed the exam although he's very intelligent.

....

3 Read the paragraph below, and write sentences saying what might/could have happened to Agatha Christie.

On the night of 3 December 1926, the famous author Agatha Christie disappeared from her home near London. On 14 December, after a nationwide search, she was recognised by the head waiter at a hotel in Yorkshire. She had been missing for 11 days, and what actually happened to her during that time still remains a mystery.

1 The police suggested that she had been in a car accident.

....

2 Journalists wondered if she had disappeared to get publicity.

....

3 Her husband thought she had lost her memory.

....

4 Perhaps she decided to have a holiday on her own.

....

5 Maybe she had argued with her husband.

....

6 Some people believed she had a nervous breakdown.

....

4 Read the story and decide whether you think it is true.

5 Answer the questions.

1 Why were the upper floors of the skyscrapers *invisible?*

....

2 The windows were *opaque.* So could the office workers see through the windows or not?

....

3 'But *they* were used to *it.*' Who were *they* and what were they used to?

....

4 '. . . she was looking forward to the *reunion* over the weekend.' The *reunion* with whom?

....

5 '. . . she let one of her *regulars* off . . .' What does *regulars* mean?

....

6 Why did she pull the emergency handle?

....

7 Why was there no response?

....

6 How do you think the story ends?

Now turn to page 77 and find out.

7 Answer the questions.

1 How do you think Betty Lou Oliver felt when she went to work that morning?

She must have been ....

2 How do you think she felt when the accident happened?

....

3 How do you think her rescuers felt when they reached her?

....

8 Write a title for the story.

....

It happened on a foggy Saturday morning in New York, July 28th, 1945. The kind of morning when the upper floors of the skyscrappers were invisible and the 35,000 office workers who thronged the Empire State Building looked out to opaque, dripping windows. But they were used to it. When you worked in the world's tallest building, you saw a lot of clouds.

On duty that morning was an attractive 20-year-old lift operator called Betty Lou Oliver.

It was a special day for her. She had come up to New York six weeks before, to await the return of her husband from active duty in the Pacific, and had taken the job to fill in time. Today was her last day and she was looking forward to the reunion over the weekend. She had no idea how special it would be.

She liked the work. Number 6 car was one of the express lifts which served the upper floors and the long haul up and down gave her a chance to talk to the customers.

It was 9.55am, just coming up to her coffee break, when she let one of her regulars off at the 79th floor. He stopped for a moment to wish her luck and say how much he would miss her. The doors closed behind him, the lift started down and within seconds she was plunged into a living nightmare.

The lift was picking up speed as it passed the 76th floor when there was violent explosion in the shaft above and the floor seemed to drop away beneath her.

The lift car slammed against the sides of the shaft, and as she struggled to keep her feet, the ceiling just above her head burst into flames. With burning fragments falling in her hair, she pulled the emergency handle as hard as she could. There was no response, the brakes weren't working.

She had no idea what was happening. She stared at the indicator board, hypnotised by the floor numbers spinning by faster and faster . . .

Betty Lou Oliver was a victim of one of the most bizarre accidents on record. A B-25 bomber on a routine flight had got lost in the fog, and had crashed into the 79th floor of the Empire State Building. One of the engines sliced through the cables of No. 6 lift and ended up on the roof of the lift car. So it was that Betty Lou began her fall down the lift shaft, accelerating, according to the relentless laws of gravity, by 9.8 metres per second. There was nothing anyone could do.

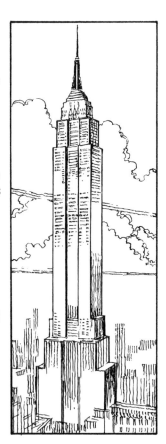

❶ Decide which lesson of Unit 6 in the Students'
Book the following words come from.

alarm bell bargain bomb college dragon
fate fees festival finals firework flag ghost
horoscope investment lift merchant
money-lender monument motorist puncture
seminar sculptor stony term vegetarian

26 **Let's celebrate**
27 **Tall stories**
28 ***A question of choice*** and ***Romeo and Juliet***
29 **Britain in View: students in higher education**
30 ***You and I are about to die***: A short story

❷ Look at the words in exercise 1 again.
Cross out any silent consonants.
Which words contain the /ə/ sound? Circle the
sound.

❸ Complete the sentences with the words in bold.

owe, borrow, lend
1 I asked the bank manager if I could .... some money to buy a car.
2 She agreed to .... me £750.
3 You gave me £5 and the bill was only £3.50 so I .... you £1.50.

burgle, steal
4 People often break into cars to .... the radio.
5 We were worried that someone might .... the house while we were away.

sensible, sensitive
6 If you've got toothache, be .... and go to the dentist.
7 He's rather .... and hates being criticised.

debt, loan
8 If you spend more than you earn, you get into ....
9 The company will have to close if it can't get a bank ....

conference, lecture
10 Professor Walton is giving a .... on archaeology this evening.
11 World leaders met at a .... in Geneva to discuss environmental problems.

chance, luck
12 There's a good .... that you'll get the job.
13 Good .... with your interview!

④ Each word in column A is different from the word opposite in column B. For example, *celebration* in column A is more general than *parade* in column B. Choose the sentence which explains the difference between each pair of words and write 1, 2, or 3 in the chart.

1 The word in column A is more general than the word in column B.

2 The word in column A means almost the same as the word in column B.

3 The word in column A means the opposite of the word in column B.

	A	B
1	celebration	parade
	friend	enemy
	scientist	biologist
	gigantic	huge
	dead	alive
	congested	crowded
	animal	rat
	worthless	priceless
	absurd	ridiculous
	complicated	simple
	qualification	degree
	mad	crazy
	instrument	drum
	propose	suggest
	ancient	modern

⑤ Check how much English you know. Answer yes (✔), not sure (?) or no (X).

Can you . . .?
use the third conditional ☐

Do you know how to . . .?
give reasons with *as, because* and *since* ☐
express purpose with *in order to* and *so that* ☐
express belief and disbelief ☐
express result with *so/such . . . that, as a result* and *consequently* ☐
talk about imaginary situations in the past ☐
express wishes for the present ☐
express regret about the past ☐
make deductions with *must/can't have* ☐
speculate with *might/could have* ☐

Do you know when to use . . .?
so . . . that and *such . . . that*
the second and third conditional ☐

If you answered *no* to any questions, look at the STRUCTURES TO LEARN in Lessons 26–30 of your Students' Book. Write sentences using the structures.

....

....

....

....

If you answered *not sure* to any questions, write sentences using the structures.

....

....

....

....

Now look at the STRUCTURES TO LEARN in Lessons 26–30 of your Students' Book and check.

⑥ Write a few sentences about:

• celebrations in your country
• something you believe in
• a choice you made, and what would(n't) have happened if you had chosen differently
• your wishes for change in the present
• a lucky event in your life

....

....

....

....

....

....

⑦ Look at the STRUCTURES TO LEARN and the WORDS TO REMEMBER in Units 4–6 of your Students' Book. Choose the five structures and the ten words which are most useful to you and write them down.

....

....

....

....

....

Lesson 6, exercise 4

Dr Jenny Palmer has been working at St Thomas's hospital for seven years. She has been looking after the Children's Department for the last five years. She has helped over two thousand children to get better. She has only had two weeks' holiday in the last two years.

Tony French has been gardening for the last 15 years, and has worked on seven gardens in country houses. Since 1987 he has been working at St Aldate's College and has planted over 500 new types of flowers in the gardens there.

Julie Dawn Rose has been writing for *The Independent* newspaper since 1991 and has written over 100 articles. For the last three months she has been doing research for an important article and has interviewed more than 50 people.

Now turn back to page 14.

Lesson 7, exercise 8

Write as much as you can remember from the passage on New York about the following:

- New York's recent past
- Its financial institutions
- Different types of industry
- Service industries
- Its economic future

....

....

....

....

....

....

....

....

....

Lesson 8, exercise 6

If your total is 45 or below, you probably have excellent resistance to stress. A score over 45 indicates some vulnerability to stress, and a score over 55 indicates serious vulnerability to stress.

Lesson 10, exercise 5

Answers
1 *ballet, performance*
2 *mingling*
3 You are *unaware* of an unwitting insult
4 Trying to begin a romantic relationship
5 An insult
6 *taxi driver*
7 *hit*
8 Watch other people's body language carefully

Unit 2 Review, exercise 5

Write down the ten words or phrases you have learnt.

....

....

....

....

....

....

....

....

....

....

Can you remember them all?

Unit 3 Review, exercise 6

Write down the ten words or phrases you have learnt.

....

....

....

....

....

....

....

Can you remember them all?

Lesson 17, exercise 1

As you can see, the owners have had a lot of work done to improve the property. Without looking back at page 40, write sentences saying what they've had done, and what they haven't had done yet.

....

....

....

....

....

....

....

....

Now turn back to page 40 and check.

Lesson 20, exercise 8

Read the second part of the story.

'Pardon me', he said. 'You're a very pretty girl.'

'Thank you', she said.

'Don't talk to him,' her mother said. 'Don't answer him. I'm warning you. Believe me.'

'I'm in love with you,' he said to the girl.

'I don't believe you,' the girl said.

'Don't answer him,' the mother said.

'I really do,' he said. 'In fact, I'm so much in love with you that I want to marry you.'

'Do you have a job?' she said.

'Yes, today is my first day. I'm going to Manhattan to start my first day of work.'

'What kind of work will you do?' she asked.

'I don't know exactly,' he said. 'You see, I didn't start yet.'

'It sounds exciting,' she said.

'It's my first job, but I'll have my own desk and handle a lot of papers and carry them around in a briefcase, and it will pay well, and I'll work my way up.'

'I love you,' she said.

'Will you marry me?'

'I don't know. You'll have to ask my mother.'

The young man rose from his seat and stood before the girl's mother. He cleared his throat very carefully for a long time. 'May I have the honor of having your daughter's hand in marriage?' he said, but he was drowned out by the subway noise.

The mother looked up at him and said, 'What?' He couldn't hear her either, but he could tell by the movement of her lips and by the way her face wrinkled up that she said, What.

The train pulled to a stop.

'May I have the honor of having your daughter's hand in marriage?' he shouted, not realising there was no subway noise. Everybody on the train looked at him, smiled, and then they all applauded.

'Are you crazy?' the mother asked.

The train started again.

'What?' he said.

'Why do you want to marry her?' she asked.

'Well, she's pretty – I mean, I'm in love with her.'

'Is that all?'

'I guess so,' he said. 'Is there supposed to be more?'

'No. Not usually,' the mother said. 'Are you working?'

'Yes. As a matter of fact, that's why I'm going into Manhattan so early. Today is the first day of my first job.'

'Congratulations,' the mother said.

'Thanks,' he said. 'Can I marry your daughter?'

'Do you have a car?' she asked.

'Not yet,' he said. 'But I should be able to get one pretty soon. And a house too.

'A house?'

'With lots of rooms.'

'Yes, that's what I expected you to say,' she said. She turned to her daughter. 'Do you love him?'

'Yes, Mother, I do.'

'Why?'

'Because he's good, and gentle, and kind.'

'Are you sure?'

'Yes.'

'Then you really love him.'

'Yes.'

'Are you sure there isn't anyone else that you might love and might want to marry?'

'No, Mother,' the girl said.

Now turn back to page 47.

Lesson 20, exercise 10

Read the last part of the story.

'Well, then,' the mother said to the young man. 'Looks like there's nothing I can do about it. Ask her again.'

The train stopped.

'My dearest one,' he said, 'will you marry me?'

'Yes,' she said.

Everybody in the car smiled and applauded.

'Isn't life wonderful?' the boy asked the mother.

'Beautiful,' the mother said.

The conductor climbed down from between the cars as the train started up and, straightening his dark tie, approached them with a solemn black book in his hand.

Why do you think the conductor approached them with a solemn black book in his hand?

Now turn back to page 47.

Unit 5 Review, exercise 5

Write down the ten words or phrases you have learnt.

....

....

....

....

....

....

....

....

Can you remember them all?

Lesson 30, exercise 6

The crash shook the foundations of the building like an explosion. The lift car went through the basement and it buried itself in the ground beneath.

Miraculously, unbelievably, Betty Lou Oliver survived. Rescuers had to tear their way through a tangled mass of debris to get at her, her back and both legs were broken, but underneath it all, she was alive.

She was taken to hospital and made a remarkable recovery in about eight months. She resumed normal life, and moved to Arkansas where she eventually raised a family and became a grandmother.

Now turn back to page 70.